ABBEYS, PRIORIES AND CATHEDRALS

BRITAIN'S HERITAGE IN CLOISTER AND CLOSE

ROMSEY ABBEY – *The Nave Looking East 1904* 51433

ABBEYS, PRIORIES AND CATHEDRALS

BRITAIN'S HERITAGE IN CLOISTER AND CLOSE

WITH PHOTOGRAPHS FROM THE FRANCIS FRITH COLLECTION

Compiled and edited by Eliza Sackett and Julia Skinner

First published in the United Kingdom in 2006 by The Francis Frith Collection

Hardback Edition ISBN 1-84589-277-1

British Library Cataloguing in Publication Data

Abbeys, Priories and Cathedrals
Compiled and edited by Eliza Sackett and Julia Skinner

The Francis Frith Collection
Frith's Barn, Teffont,
Salisbury, Wiltshire SP3 5QP
Tel: +44 (0) 1722 716 376
Email: info@francisfrith.co.uk
www.francisfrith.com

Designed and assembled by Terence Sackett
Image enhancing by Sue Molloy

Printed in Singapore by Imago

Front Cover: Worcester, The Cathedral and the River 1891 *29297t*
The colour-tinting in this book is for illustrative purposes only, and is not intended to be historically accurate.

Contents

ABBEYS, PRIORIES AND CATHEDRALS

An Introduction

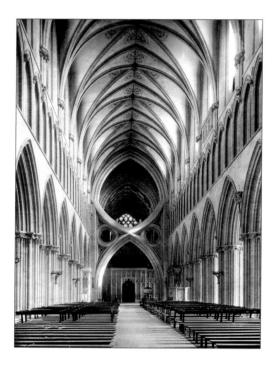

THIS BOOK is a celebration of Britain's ecclesiastical heritage in all its extraordinary diversity, from the humblest priories and abbeys to the most spectacular and magnificent cathedrals.

Many of our abbeys were modest affairs, built in remote countryside, far from the temptations of towns and cities. Here a handful of monks and friars passed their time in pious solitude; other monasteries were grander institutions, accumulating vast riches from farming and other local industries, and wielding considerable regional power. Their wealth was reflected in the splendour of their buildings, which often spread over several acres.

Today we wander the ruins of our surviving abbeys trying to piece together a picture of how they once looked. Very often only fragments of masonry remain, with markers placed on the ground to indicate where the various buildings were sited. Often it is almost impossible for us to conjure up any true impression of how life must have been for the monks who passed their days there. We see these monastic buildings as plain architectural ruins, their former glories and deep spiritual associations long gone. However, as Abbot Gasquet points out in his 'English Monastic Life' (1904), to the monks of the monastic era every single stone in their abbey was a testament to God: 'To the builders of these old sanctuaries the work was one of faith and love rather than a matter of mere mercenary business. They designed and worshipped whilst they wrought. To them, says one writer, the building "was instinct with speech, a tree of life planted in paradise; sending its roots deep down into the crypt; rising with stems in pillar and shaft; branching out into boughs over the vaulting; blossoming in diaper and mural flora; breaking out into foliage, flower, and fruit, on corbel, capital, and boss". It was all real and true to them, for it sprang out of their strong belief that in the church they had "the House of God" and "the Gate of Heaven", into which at the moment of the solemn dedication "the King of Glory" had come to take lasting possession of His home.'

The word 'monk' derives from the Greek 'monachos', meaning 'alone'. True monasticism arose in Europe at the end of the 5th century after St Benedict founded a monastery in Italy. His Benedictine rules for religious communities have been the foundation for monastic life ever since. The first monks were hermits, who led solitary, ascetic lives, often in simple cells set close by water or near the sea. In Britain, the Celtic Church remained influential, especially in the north, but St Augustine brought the rule of St Benedict to southern Britain in AD597. Later, King Alfred and St Dunstan encouraged the growth of Benedictine monasteries. After the Norman Conquest more monasteries were founded, and various monastic orders developed. By the time of the Black Death (1348–49) monasticism in Britain was at its peak, with over 1,000 monasteries, about 14,000 monks, and about 3,000 nuns. The causes of the decline of the monasteries are complex. The Black Death played a part; so did the rise of a wealthy middle class – careers other than the religious life became available, and rich merchants tended to endow their parish church, not the monasteries. Henry VIII was one of the main causes of the decline in monasteries. His momentous decision to break with the Church of Rome set into motion the abrupt breakup of the monastic way of life. His agents immediately embarked on the dismantling process, demolishing abbey after abbey (although some abbey churches were saved by becoming the local parish church). Without the constant stewardship of the abbots and monks, the monastic buildings rapidly declined and deteriorated; some were plundered by local farmers and landowners for building stone, and many a fragment of carved stone from an abbey arch or ceiling can be found lodged in a farmhouse wall.

A cathedral contains a bishop's throne (from the Greek and Latin 'cathedra', meaning chair or throne), and is thus the building where the principal churchman in the diocese has his chair of office. Our cathedrals were built to the glory of God, clear, unequivocal affirmations of the power of the established church over the people. The growth of cathedrals was directly allied to the development of monasteries. Some, indeed, were originally united to monasteries, an arrangement initiated by the Normans; these include Wells, Winchester, Worcester, Canterbury, Rochester, Durham, Bath, Norwich and Ely. Other cathedrals were managed by canons, some of whom lived in monastic style, and some of whom were secular. Their cathedrals included Carlisle, Bristol, Oxford, London, York, Lichfield, Hereford, Exeter, Lincoln, Chichester, and Salisbury. After the Dissolution, Henry VIII created more cathedrals, including Westminster (demoted in 1550), Peterborough, Gloucester, and Chester, which all used old Benedictine abbey churches. No new cathedrals were created in England between 1546 and 1836. Over twenty cathedrals have been created since then, some using the existing parish church, some using newly-built buildings, and some using originally monastic churches – these last include St Albans, Ripon, and Southwell.

This book offers the reader a unique survey, for the finely detailed period photographs, specially selected from the world-famous Francis Frith Collection, mostly picture our abbeys, priories and cathedrals as they were before 20th-century conservation bodies tidied and restored them. This vital restoration work, of course, secured them for future generations, but in the case of many of the smaller abbeys it inevitably removed much of their romance. Many of the Frith historical scenes, taken in the late 19th century, reveal these ecclesiastical buildings as they looked at a time when ruins were considered a direct source of the Sublime, and fit objects for poetical contemplation. The medieval architects, of course, would have been horrified to see such ruins, and shocked at the decline of the buildings they had so painstakingly and lovingly created all those centuries ago. However, for us the book offers a unique opportunity to experience our religious buildings as they were in a past era, before they were tidied, extended or altered.

The quotations from celebrated writers, poets and travellers down the centuries add to the authentic atmosphere, offering us invaluable impressions of how our cathedrals and abbeys were viewed by previous ages and generations. Invariably vividly written, they are often unexpectedly outspoken.

This pictorial survey should leave every one of us astonished at the sheer wealth of our surviving ecclesiastical heritage. Let us hope it encourages us to continue to protect our historic buildings now and into the future.

EXETER CATHEDRAL

The pride of Exeter is its magnificent cathedral, famed for its stone sculpture and woodcarvings, the bishop's throne, the astronomical clock, the twin Norman towers, the wonderful vaulted roof and many other treasures. During the Second World War the cathedral suffered from the effects of a

500lb bomb, which demolished three bays of the south choir aisle. Luckily much of the precious ancient glass and portable objects had previously been moved to a place of safety; the damage to the cathedral was repaired, and the valuables were eventually returned.

The work on the magnificent west front of Exeter Cathedral (opposite page and left) dates from about 1329 to 1342, although there is some Norman work as well. A statue of St Peter, the patron saint, is located high on the gable. A detailed study of the carvings reveals English kings, priests and soldiers. Note the kings sitting cross-legged. Angels, prophets and apostles are also depicted by those long-dead craftsmen.

Exeter Cathedral is the only cathedral in England that does not have a central tower; this allows the roof to run uninterrupted from end to end of the building, making it the longest stretch of Gothic vaulting in the world. The soaring grandeur of the vaulting, the great choir screen, and the organ case are the main features of the magnificent view of the nave shown on the right. The sheer scale of the work and the skill shown by craftsmen almost 700 years ago is still awe-inspiring.

WAX VOTIVE FIGURES

When repairs to the cathedral were being made after bomb damage in 1943, a collection of wax models was found in a cavity of a stone screen above Bishop Lacy's tomb. These models were mainly of human and animal limbs, but there was also a complete figure of a woman. It is thought they were offerings given by pilgrims at the tomb of Bishop Edmund Lacy, pilgrims who had come to pray for the recovery of either themselves, of members of their family, or of sick animals. These votive figures are now kept in the Cathedral Library. Bishop Edmund Lacy was a distinguished figure. As Dean of the Royal Chapel, Lacy accompanied Henry V to the battle of Agincourt in 1415; he was appointed Bishop of Exeter in 1420, and immediately, says the Rev George Oliver in his 'Lives of the Bishops of Exeter' (1861), showed 'zeal in promoting the completion of his cathedral and its cloisters'. After his death in 1455, 'the bishop's memory was long venerated in this diocese', says Oliver, and 'pilgrims resorted to his tomb'.

Top: EXETER, FROM THE CANAL 1896   38033

Above: EXETER CATHEDRAL, THE NAVE LOOKING EAST 1896   37998

Above: EXETER CATHEDRAL, THE WEST FRONT 1924   76587A

The little broken-visaged effigies of saints and kings and bishops, niched in tiers along this hoary wall, are prodigiously black and quaint and primitive in expression; and as you look at them with whatever contemplative tenderness your trade of hard-working tourist may have left at your disposal, you fancy that they are broodingly conscious of their names, histories and misfortunes; that, sensitive victims of time, they feel the loss of their noses, their toes, and their crowns; and that, when the long June twilight turns at last to a deeper gray and the quiet of the close to a deeper stillness, they begin to peer sidewise out of their narrow recesses and to converse in some strange form of early English, as rigid, yet as candid, as their features and postures, moaning, like a company of ancient paupers round a hospital fire, over their aches and infirmities and losses, and the sadness of being so terribly old.

HENRY JAMES, 1872

Among the few remains of religious houses in North Devon are those of the Augustinian priory at Frithelstock, a daughter house of Hartland Abbey in the north-west corner of Devon, founded c1220 by Robert de Beauchamp, and dissolved in 1536. All that is now left are the remnants of walls of the priory church, although there are three fine lancet windows in the west wall. In 1845, not that long before this photograph was taken, there was more of the priory to see: W G Hoskins, in his 'Devon', tells how Sir Stephen Glynne saw remains of a church tower and the refectory, which had 'a fine open roof … with collar and hammer beams'. Next to the ruins stands the 15th-century parish church.

Left: TORRINGTON, FRITHELSTOCK PRIORY AND CHURCH 1893   32317

Its bells must answer those of Monkleigh across the little valley; its pride is the ruined priory that has seen seven centuries come and go. Its fine west wall still stands proudly with three lancet windows and an ancient doorway. Forty feet high it is, and (they told us) not more than an inch out of true … Who would not enjoy walking to church on Sunday down the fine avenue of limes in this churchyard?

ARTHUR MEE,
'THE KING'S ENGLAND, DEVON', 1938

FRITHELSTOCK PRIORY

DUNSTER PRIORY

The extraordinary building (left) at the south end of Dunster's High Street is 14th-century, and was formerly known as the Chantry of St Lawrence. It acted as a guest house for visitors to the priory. It acquired its present soubriquet around 1769.

St George's Church (below) was originally the church for Dunster's Benedictine priory, which was founded in the 11th century.

Left:
DUNSTER,
THE NUNNERY 1903
50477

Below:
DUNSTER, THE
DOVECOTE AND THE
PRIORY CHURCH 1919
69262

 DUNSTER PRIORY'S DOVECOTE

The round building in 69262 is a dovecote. There were once about 26,000 dovecotes like this in Britain; the ones that remain seem picturesque to us now, but in fact they were an early form of factory farming. The monks kept up to 500 pigeons in here, which were killed for food, and provided a constant source of fresh meat. This was especially welcome in the winter months, for until relatively recently, all animals were slaughtered in November and their meat 'preserved'; in fact, in the days before frozen foods, much meat was past its best by the spring. The nest boxes for the pigeons were in the thick walls of the dovecote, and they were accessed by a revolving ladder – its massive central post was called a potence. The pigeons' droppings were also very useful as fertiliser. This dovecote, a rare survival, was restored in 1989.

CLEEVE ABBEY

'Is not this place haunted?' asked a visitor to Cleeve.
'Only by the good', replied Cleeva Clapp, who spent her life at this
ancient Somerset Cistercian abbey in the early 1900s.

Cleeve is indeed atmospheric: many of its buildings are still so
complete that the centuries quickly fall away, and you feel the
presence of the white-habited, silent monks who paced its cloisters
five hundred years ago.

Henry VIII destroyed Cleeve's abbey church at the Dissolution.
Later, one of the buildings was converted into a farmhouse, part of
the cloisters into a cottage, and the central garden into a farmyard.
Manure steamed in heaps in the chapter house, and a stone wall
across the centre of the court kept the pigs and sheep apart.

In 1875, the Luttrells of Dunster Castle, who owned Cleeve
Abbey, began a programme of restoration. The farmhouse was
converted into three cottages, and Cleeva Clapp – named after the
abbey – lived in one of them. She had a passion for this ancient
ruin that lasted throughout her life, which was spent giving guided
tours. The plot of ground outside the refectory was turned into a
market garden. The picture of the refectory (below right) shows her
vegetable patch. Cleeva sold cream teas and enthused to everyone,
deeply in love with her building.

Cleeve is remarkable in that although nothing can be seen of
the abbey church except its excavated foundations, the rest of the
abbey buildings are in an excellent state (after the Dissolution they
were used as farm buildings and kept in good repair). This means
that at Cleeve it is relatively easy for the visitor to grasp the typical
layout of a Cistercian abbey and to imagine what the daily life of
a monk might be like. In photograph 27523 (below right) we are
looking at the south range from outside the cloister. On the first
floor are the splendid windows of the new refectory, created in
the 15th century; this beautiful room has an ornate timber roof
supported by carved angel corbels. Below are the much smaller
windows of bedrooms and studies used by senior monks towards
the end of the abbey's life.

The photograph above right shows the impressive gateway
entrance to Cleeve Abbey. This was built in the 13th century, and
was altered and enlarged in the 14th and 16th centuries.

The photograph opposite looks through the lay brothers' part
of the abbey across the cloister garth to the east range. A door at
the extreme left leads to the library, an unusual feature. The ornate
window belongs to the chapter house; then comes the day stair to
the dorter above, which stretches the whole length of the range and
is lit by the lancet windows. Today, the future of Cleeve is assured,
as English Heritage is responsible for its upkeep. In 1998 the abbey
celebrated its 800th anniversary.

Opposite: OLD CLEEVE, CLEEVE ABBEY 1938   88728
Above left: OLD CLEEVE, CLEEVE ABBEY, THE GATEHOUSE 1935   86615
Above right: OLD CLEEVE, CLEEVE ABBEY, MEDIEVAL TILES
Below: OLD CLEEVE, CLEEVE ABBEY, THE REFECTORY 1890   27523

GLASTONBURY ABBEY

Tradition says that Glastonbury's abbey might date from the time of British Christianity before Somerset was conquered by the Saxons, but it was probably founded by King Ine of Wessex in the early 8th century. The most influential person in the early development of the abbey was Dunstan, born nearby at Baltonsborough, and abbot from AD940 to AD956. He extended the buildings and reformed the monks' lifestyle with the introduction of the rule of St Benedict.

In 1184 fire destroyed most of the building, and almost the whole complex had to be rebuilt. The date of rebuilding is usually given as 1186, although in reality it must have been spread over several years. The abbey, and its abbots, grew increasingly wealthy over the centuries, and Glastonbury was one of the main targets of Henry VIII's Dissolution of the Monasteries in the 1530s.

In the above photograph the chapel of St Thomas the Martyr (better known as Thomas à Becket) is through the archway to the left. The main difference today, apart from the dress of the visitors such as the couple seen here, is the presence of a path and concrete outlines to show where walls used to be.

Richard Whyting, the last abbot, was tried for treason (probably for his support of Queen Katherine in the matter of Henry VIII's divorce), and was hanged, drawn and quartered on Glastonbury Tor. Thereafter much of the stonework of the abandoned abbey was robbed for re-use elsewhere. In 1907 the site was bought on behalf of the Church of England.

In the photograph (below left) we see the Benediction being given by the bishop in the abbey ruins around the turn of the 20th century.

But in so far as beauty of structure is beauty of line and curve, balance and harmony of masses and dimensions, I have seldom relished it as deeply as on the grassy nave of some crumbling church, before lonely columns and empty windows where the wild flowers were a cornice and the sailing clouds a roof. The arts certainly hang together in what they do for us. These hoary relics of Glastonbury reminded me in their broken eloquence of one of the other great ruins of the world – the Last Supper of Leonardo. A beautiful shadow, in each case, is all that remains; but that shadow is the soul of the artist.

HENRY JAMES, 1872

Opposite left: GLASTONBURY ABBEY, THE TRANSEPT ARCHES 1912 64486P

Opposite right: GLASTONBURY ABBEY, ST JOSEPH'S CHAPEL DOORWAY 1912 64482

Left: GLASTONBURY ABBEY, THE BENEDICTION BY THE PRIMATE C1900 G12340

BEAN SOUP

Upon the sign for vespers, after making their prayer, the cooks were to proceed to the kitchen and obtain the necessary measure of beans for the following day. They then said their vespers together, and proceeded to wash the beans in three waters … The pot was to be watched most carefully lest the contents should be burnt. The skins were to be taken off as they became loosened, and the beans were to be removed as they were cooked … When the cooking of this bean soup had progressed so far, the four cooks were to sit down and say their Divine Office together whilst the hot water was being boiled. A third pot, with vegetables in cold water, was to be then made ready to take its place on the fire, after the Gospel of the morning Mass. When the daily Chapter was finished, the beans were again to be put on the fire and boiled with more water … Two of the four weekly cooks now went to the High Mass, the other two remaining behind to watch the dinner … When the community were ready for their meal, the first cook ladled out the soup into dishes, and the other three carried them to the refectory. ABBOT GASQUET, 1904

The abbot's kitchen (above and below) dates from the 14th century. It is not only the best preserved building of the abbey, but also one of the best preserved medieval kitchens in Europe. It was well designed for its purpose, being square-sided, with the roof angled to take heat and smoke from cookery up and out through the louvres at the top of the conical roof. It is said to have been erected by Abbot Chinnock, who governed the monastery from 1374 to 1420.

Above right:
GLASTONBURY
ABBEY, THE ABBOT'S
KITCHEN 1912 64484

Right:
GLASTONBURY
ABBEY, THE ABBOT'S
KITCHEN 1890 23917

Abandoned and allowed to fall into ruins, it soon became regarded as the common stone-quarry of the neighbourhood … Between 1792 to 1794, the ground surrounding it was cleared, levelled, and converted into pasturage; and cart-loads of stones, capitals, corbels, pinnacles, and rich fragments of sculpture were used for making a new road over the marshes to Wells. VICTORIAN GUIDEBOOK

WELLS CATHEDRAL

But Wells is in fact not a city with a cathedral for central feature; it is a cathedral with a little city gathered at the base and forming hardly more than an extension of the spacious close. You feel everywhere the presence of the beautiful church; the place seems always to savour of a Sunday afternoon; and you imagine every house tenanted by a canon, a prebendary or a precentor, with 'backs' providing for choristers and vergers.

HENRY JAMES, 1872

The present cathedral was begun in 1190; it was built in oolitic limestone from Glastonbury Abbey's quarry at Doulting – the stone is still being quarried today. It is the first cathedral built completely in the English Gothic style. Between 1314 and 1438 the central tower was raised to its present height and topped with a spire. The north-west tower was added in 1430. The south-west tower was built in 1380, and contains the heaviest ring of ten bells in the world. Wells Cathedral is famous for its stone carvings, particularly on its west front, which date from about 1230. Christ in glory reigns at the top; beneath him are the twelve apostles, then the ten orders of angels; the row beneath contains the souls rising from the dead, lifting their tombstone lids; in the next row are bishops, kings, knights, saints, martyrs and virgins. The lower niches to the north contain scenes from the New Testament, and to the south scenes from the Old Testament, while beneath these are angels. Over the central door is the coronation of the Virgin, and beneath it a statue of the Virgin and child. During festival processions around the churchyard, the illiterate peasant would gaze up at the 300 medieval statues (which were all originally colourfully painted), entranced by the trumpet blasts and celestial singing issuing from the holes beneath the great west window, where the back wall of the anterior passage acts as a sounding board, imagining the glory of the Day of Judgement when he would pass on to the joys of Paradise. The tradition of stone carving continues: Robert Aldridge carved the head of Master Mason Bert Wheeler (1935–1978) wearing spectacles, which was added to the Chapter House roof, and the head of the groundsman Charlie Clark, with his cloth cap and coal sack. By the north porch stand symbols of the four evangelists: the angel of St Matthew, the eagle of St John, the ox of St Luke and the lion of St Mark were carved in Doulting stone by Mary Spencer Watson, and presented to Wells Cathedral by the Jerusalem Trust in 1995.

Left: WELLS CATHEDRAL 1890   23870

Above: WELLS CATHEDRAL, THE NAVE LOOKING EAST 1890   23878

Above: WELLS CATHEDRAL, THE CHAPTER HOUSE C1945   W47016

Below: WELLS CATHEDRAL, THE CATHEDRAL CLOCK 1906   55156

The beautiful curve of the steps on the right is for all the world like the surge of a great wave that will presently break and subside into smaller ones like those at the top of the picture. It is one of the most imaginative lines it has been my good fortune to try and depict, this superb mounting of the steps. . . .

FREDERICK EVANS, 1903

Above left: WELLS CATHEDRAL, THE STEPS TO THE CHAPTER HOUSE
C1900 W47301

Above right: WELLS CATHEDRAL, THE BISHOP'S PALACE, THE RUINS
1890 23896

The innovative 14th-century scissor arches are the most striking aspect of the nave (23878, opposite far left). Some visitors imagine that the scissor arches are modern, but they were added in 1340 under the central tower in order to give it extra support: the additional weight of the spire and the fact that the cathedral was built so close to water springs caused the tower to tilt. In 1438 the tower burnt down, but the arches remain. Today the benches have gone; the altar stands in front of the arches, surrounded by elegant limed oak seats installed in 1997.

Bishop Burnell built the great palace in about 1290 (above right). It was ruined in the 16th century when Sir John Gates purchased its timber, lead and glass. In the 19th century Bishop Law destroyed part of the Banqueting Hall so as to have a fashionable ruin in his garden. It has since served as a dramatic backdrop to concerts and plays.

Photograph 55156 (opposite below) shows the outside dial of Wells Cathedral's famous medieval clock. The figures and face of the outside clock are 100 years later than those inside. The bells are struck by the knights on the quarter hour. The inscription 'Nequid pereat' is a quotation from St John's Gospel, and means 'Let nothing perish (or be lost)', referring to the church fabric and the passage of time.

The roundels to the left of the beautiful, undulating 13th-century steps in W47301 (above left) contain some of the oldest medieval glass in the cathedral. The steps veer elegantly to the right to the chapter house, and extend ahead over the 15th-century chain gate. The steps were beautifully photographed and described by the architectural photographer Frederick Evans in 1903, in an image taken from a similar viewpoint to the Frith photograph.

BRISTOL CATHEDRAL

Bristol Cathedral is sited a little away from the city centre, so that it retains some of the quiet atmosphere we associate with medieval times (24635p, above). It was originally an Augustinian abbey, founded c1140. It was one of the six monasteries designated as cathedrals by Henry VIII at the Dissolution, thus preserving a remarkable building. Because it lacks a clerestory and triforium, the aisles of Bristol Cathedral rise to the same height as the nave, a feature making it unique among English cathedrals; the vast pillared area glows with light. The original Norman nave was partially reconstructed at the time of the Dissolution, but then was allowed to fall into ruin. The present nave, brilliantly designed by G E Street to blend imperceptibly with the older part of the cathedral, was built, along with the west towers, between 1868 and 1888. The reredos was erected in 1899, and is renowned for its skeleton vaulting and stellate tomb recesses. Many of the monastic buildings survive, including the richly decorated chapter house; others are now incorporated into the Cathedral School.

The effect is very striking … We have before us a lengthened avenue of arcading, as remarkable for its solemnity as for its beauty. Though the vault is only 52 feet above the floor, there is no feeling of depression. This is due perhaps to the form of arch, not flattened, as at Lincoln and York, but boldly pointed, and springing directly, not from a triforium, but from the pavement.

J P NORRIS, 1884

Opposite: BRISTOL CATHEDRAL 1890   24635P

Above: BRISTOL, A PANORAMIC VIEW OF THE CITY AND THE CATHEDRAL 1900   45563

Left: BRISTOL CATHEDRAL, THE NAVE LOOKING EAST 1900   45572

Has any English town a fairer scene than this? … On one side flows the rivulet, so shallow and crystal clear that every polished pebble of its bed gleams in the sun … Against the sky stand out the pinnacled tower and the long lines of the priory roof.

ARTHUR MEE, 'THE KING'S ENGLAND, HAMPSHIRE', 1939

CHRISTCHURCH PRIORY

This is possibly the finest example in Britain of a complete church of Augustinian canons still in use for worship. (It was first built for secular canons; then in 1149 Baldwin de Redvers, 1st Earl of Devon, and Lord of the Manor of Christchurch, introduced 26 Augustinian monks to the priory. The married lay canons were evicted, and the celibate Austins took over.) The priory nave was begun in 1094, and added to the west end of an earlier Saxon minster. The transepts were built during the reign of Henry I, and the triforium in the reign of his grandson, Henry II. The priory once had a central tower, which fell in the 12th century.

In the Middle Ages churches were places full of colour, with painted walls and ceilings. Churches could also contain pagan symbols like the Green Man – there is one in Christchurch Priory. There are also pagan images on the misericords and bench ends inside the choir. One example is a carving known as 'the Wild Man', which shows a nude male figure with a club in his right hand, like the Cerne Giant chalk hill figure in Dorset. In the left hand is a shield with a face upon it.

Christchurch Priory was famous for an unusual relic, the Miraculous Beam, which can still be seen. This was a beam for the construction of the nave; to the dismay of the builders it was found to be too short. However, the following morning it had miraculously been lengthened and fitted perfectly. The monks also told the story of a silent carpenter who worked on the church, yet never appeared for his wages.

Left: CHRISTCHURCH, THE PRIORY CHURCH AND THE RIVER AVON FROM THE TOWN BRIDGE 1906   55904

Above: CHRISTCHURCH, THE PRIORY CHURCH 1890   25203

Left:
CHRISTCHURCH, THE PRIORY CHURCH,
THE NORTH CHOIR AISLE AND THE
SALISBURY CHANTRY 1890   25219

Above:
CHRISTCHURCH, THE PRIORY CHURCH,
THE JESSE SCREEN 1918   68048

Opposite above:
CHRISTCHURCH, THE PRIORY CHURCH,
THE SHELLEY MONUMENT 1918   68050

Opposite below: CHRISTCHURCH,
THE PRIORY CHURCH, THE TRIFORIUM
1892   31383

The Lady Chapel, at the east end of the church, was completed about 1390 and vaulted about 50 years later. In 1460 the tomb of Sir John and Lady Chideoke was installed, seen below the window in photograph 25219 (above). Scrapings were taken from it to mix with water as a cure for eye problems. The Salisbury chantry (to the right) is an admirable example of the late Perpendicular style.

TO THE MEMORY OF
PERCY BYSSHE SHELLEY,
POET,
BORN AT FIELD PLACE IN THE COUNTY OF SUSSEX, AUGUST 4, 1792,
DROWNED BY THE UPSETTING OF HIS BOAT IN THE GULF OF SPEZZIA JULY, 1822.
HIS ASHES ARE INTERRED IN THE PROTESTANT BURIAL GROUND AT ROME.
ALSO TO THE MEMORY OF
MARY WOLLSTONECRAFT SHELLEY, HIS WIFE,
BORN AUGUST 30, 1797. DIED FEBRUARY 1, 1851.
HER REMAINS ARE INTERRED TOGETHER WITH THOSE OF HER FATHER WILLIAM GODWIN,
AND HER MOTHER MARY WOLLSTONECRAFT GODWIN,
IN THE CHURCHYARD AT BOURNEMOUTH.

BLAZING COLOUR

In the Middle Ages churches were a riot of colour. Christchurch Priory was painted inside: the aisle ceilings represented blue skies shining with stars, and the piers blazed with vivid colours. The illiterate laity were taught through stories, pictures and even sculptures; Pope Gregory the Great said that 'painting can do for the illiterate what writing does for those who read'. When they were first built, church walls were painted (or sometimes hung with tapestries), and the statues of the saints were painted and gilded. Most British church wall painting dates from the Norman Conquest to the Reformation; the Victorians revived it to a certain extent. Medieval paints were mostly made from earth pigments in shades of red and ochre, along with black and white. Blues were rare because they were expensive – ultramarine, made from lapis lazuli, cost more than gold leaf. Medieval artists painted straight onto the wall, which would have been prepared with size or a thin skim of plaster. Fresco (working on wet plaster) is extremely rare in Britain. The subject matter of the paintings included Bible stories, the lives of the saints, and 'moralities', or didactic fables. Churches, walls and ceilings were also decorated with patterns – diaper patterns, scrollwork, and leaf patterns were common. The photograph above shows traces of original pigment remaining on a medieval carving.

Photograph 31383 (below right) shows the north side of the nave – we are looking north-west. This is an exceptionally fine example of Norman architecture, with a sturdy arcade of grouped columns supporting a splendid triforium, all rich with deep mouldings and decorative carving. Remains of medieval wall paint exist, a reminder of a time when churches were ablaze with colour.

The east end (68048, opposite right), which has no east window, is closed by this beautiful reredos, carved in about 1360, depicting the tree of Jesse – in other words, the family tree of Jesus. The empty niches would once have held wooden statues covered with silver gilt. Behind the camera is an exceptionally fine pulpitum, or screen, of the late 14th century. The pulpitum divided the choir, the monks' part of the church, from the lay congregation.

The exquisite Shelley monument (68050, above) under the tower was designed by Henry Weekes. It commemorates the poet Shelley, who was drowned off the coast of Italy in 1822. We see the poet reclining on his wife's knee. Below are carved the lines Shelley himself wrote for his fellow poet John Keats, who also died tragically young:

He has outsoared the shadow of our night,
Envy and calumny, and hate and pain,
And that unrest which men miscall delight,
Can touch him not and torture not again.

ABBOTSBURY, ST PETER'S ABBEY

One is impressed by its ancient character. The cottages are old, stone-built and thatched; older still is the church with its grey square tower, and all about are scattered the memorials of antiquity – the chantry on the hill, standing conspicuous alone, apart, above the world; the vast old abbey barn, and rough thick stone walls, ivy-draped and crowned with beautiful valerian, and other fragments that were once parts of a great religious house. W H HUDSON, 1909

Top: ABBOTSBURY, THE TITHE BARN 1890   27322

Above: ABBOTSBURY, THE SWANNERY C1955   A2041

Abbotsbury, situated at the western end of Chesil Beach, is most famous for its swannery; the waters of the Fleet are often white with hundreds of birds. But Abbotsbury, as the name suggests, had connections with early religious life in England. St Peter's Abbey, founded for nuns in about 1023 by Orc, a Danish servant of King Canute and his wife Thola, superseded a Saxon church here. The abbey was taken over by Benedictine monks from Cerne in 1044, and thrived for 500 years until its destruction at the time of the Reformation. Only a few ruins and the tithe barn now remain. The great tithe barn was built about 1400. It has 23 bays, which are now in thatch instead of roofed with the original stone slates. Added together they give a length of 276 feet, which makes this the longest ecclesiastical barn in the country.

The monks of Abbotsbury established their swannery in about 1393, which was the year in which the swans were first given legal protection as royal birds. They provided a dependable source of feast-day meat. The swannery still exists, located on the banks of the Fleet, a lagoon cut off from the sea by the 18 miles of Chesil Beach, a huge bank of pebbles. Here hundreds of mute swans nest every year, and in May and June up to 1,000 cygnets hatch out – by October they are learning to fly.

MALMESBURY ABBEY

Top: MALMESBURY ABBEY 1924   76149
Above: MALMESBURY ABBEY 1924   76151

In the 7th century Mailduib (Maildulph), an Irish monk or hermit, settled in Malmesbury and founded a monastic school. The name Malmesbury may originally have been derived from his name. One of his pupils was Aldhelm (AD639–AD709), a most learned man; he founded the Benedictine monastery at Malmesbury around AD675 and became its first abbot. Aldhelm was revered as a saint, and was buried in Malmesbury Abbey cAD709. In about AD837 King Aethelwulf of Wessex made a shrine in the abbey for St Aldhelm's remains, and the abbey became a focus for pilgrimage. King Athelstan, grandson of Alfred the Great and the first king of a united England, is reputed to have been buried in Malmesbury Abbey cAD939.

The abbey that we can see today dates from the late 12th century and was built in the Norman style (c1150–1190), with some parts of the abbey being re-built later in the Decorated style. In the late 12th century the newly built abbey was consecrated. It had a lantern tower surmounted by a spire, which was reputed to be higher than that of Salisbury Cathedral; however, in 1479 the spire fell during a storm, causing damage to the east end of the abbey. Further damage occurred when the west tower fell in the 17th century and demolished three bays of the nave. Only a third of the original abbey remains today. After the Dissolution the abbey and the monastic buildings were eventually purchased by William Stumpe, a wealthy clothier of the town. The nave of the abbey became Malmesbury's parish church, replacing the ruined St Paul's Church. The other buildings were used as workshops for William Stumpe's looms.

The abbey has undergone various restorations. In 1928 the newly restored abbey was re-opened and re-hallowed. Today Malmesbury Abbey is still a powerful spiritual influence in the town, as it has been for centuries. Malmesbury Abbey's unique south porch (76153, right), dating from the mid 12th century and built in the Romanesque style, is decorated with 38 fine sculptures depicting detailed and elaborate images, some of which are based on Biblical scenes from both the Old and New Testaments. The images are divided by columns with decorative patterns.

Right:
MALMESBURY ABBEY,
THE SOUTH PORCH 1924
76153

EILMER, THE FLYING MONK

The library at the abbey was renowned throughout Europe during the lifetime of the historian William of Malmesbury (c1095–c1143), and indeed before then. William was famous for his 'De Gesta Regum Anglorum' ('The Deeds of the King of England'), and 'De Gesta Pontificum Anglorum' ('The Deeds of the Bishops of England'). In 'De Gesta Regum Anglorum' William tells the story of Eilmer, the flying monk of Malmesbury. Eilmer, a young monk at the abbey in the early 11th century, was interested in mathematics, astrology and the mechanics of flight. He made some wings and jumped from a tower, and is reputed to have flown some reasonable distance ('spatio stadii', the length of a stadium, perhaps about 200 metres), but he broke both legs when he crashed to the ground – he is said to have regretted that he did not make himself a tail. However, he survived his injuries and lived to a healthy old age. Eilmer is commemorated by a modern stained glass window in the abbey.

Reproduced with the kind permission of Malmesbury Abbey

FOX TALBOT, THE FATHER OF PHOTOGRAPHY

Lacock was the home of William Henry Fox Talbot, who lived from 1800 to 1877. Talbot's importance is that he established the basis of the photographic process that is still used today, the negative-positive system – an essentially reproductive process. It is not only books, prints and posters that use this process; the printed circuit boards of modern computers are miniaturised by

photo-polymerisation. The idea of photography came to Talbot when he was on holiday at Lake Como; he was using a camera lucida as an aid to drawing the scenery, and the thought came to him ' … how charming it would be if it were possible to cause these natural images to imprint themselves durably and remain fixed upon the paper'. The result of his researches was the earliest known photographic negative on paper, taken in 1835 and showing an oriel window at Lacock Abbey. Talbot called his photographic process the Calotype, from the Greek 'kalos' meaning 'beautiful'. There is now a museum at Lacock dedicated to 'the Father of Modern Photography'.

Lacock Abbey is one of our national treasures. It was founded in the early 13th century as an Augustinian nunnery by Ela, Countess of Salisbury. Ela was the wife of one of the most powerful barons of that time, William Longspee, an illegitimate son of Henry II. Lacock was one of two establishments founded by Ela in her husband's memory, the other being at Hinton Charterhouse, for Carthusian monks. The building was converted to a private residence after the Dissolution, but the cloisters, sacristy, chapter house and monastic rooms of the abbey have survived largely intact. Lacock is now much used as a location for film and television, including the 'Harry Potter' series. The photograph shows the south front to the right, originally the north wall of the abbey church, now pierced by oriel windows of c1830. A door below one of these leads to the cloister. In the centre of the west front is the 18th-century Gothick hall; to its left is the monks' kitchen.

LACOCK ABBEY

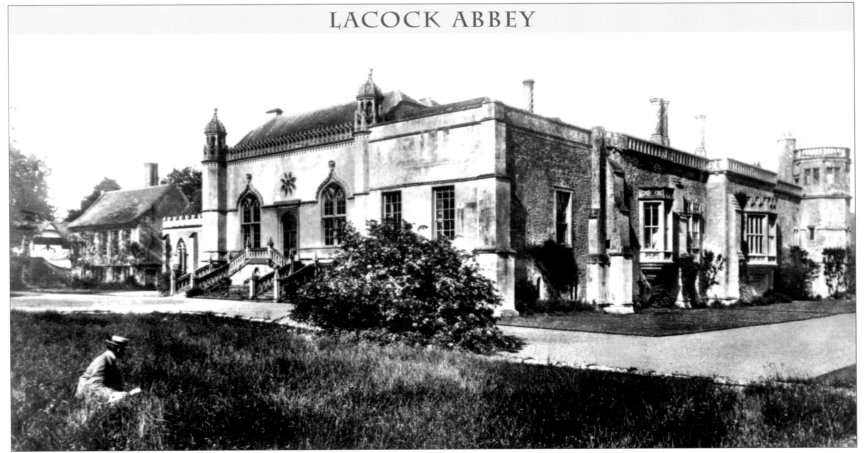

Above: LACOCK ABBEY 1904   51510P

The two photographs to the left show scenes from the Lacock Abbey Pageant of 3 September 1932. Photograph L1509p demonstrates how the medieval atmosphere at Lacock has endured to this day. The wide Perpendicular windows filter the light, and the lierne vaulting springs from slim shafts. The visitor today can still pace the cloisters as the nuns used to do, and see the sacristy, the chapter house, and the warming room.

Far left: LACOCK ABBEY, THE CLOISTERS 1932 L1509P

Left: LACOCK ABBEY, THE PAGEANT 1932 L1510

Below: LACOCK ABBEY C1955 L1026

SALISBURY CATHEDRAL

Right:
SALISBURY
CATHEDRAL FROM
THE RIVER 1887
19730

Below:
SALISBURY
CATHEDRAL, THE
NAVE LOOKING
EAST 1887   19758

Opposite:
SALISBURY,
ST ANN'S GATE
1906   56367P

I [gazed] up at the immense pile with its central soaring spire ... I could admire, even reverence, but could not love ... Occasionally I met and talked with an old man employed at the cathedral. One day, closing one eye and shading the other with his hand, he gazed up at the building for some time, and then remarked: 'I'll tell you what's wrong with Salisbury – it looks too noo'. He was near the mark; the fault is that to the professional eye it is faultless; the lack of expression is due to the fact that it came complete from its maker's brain, like a coin from the mint, and being all in one symmetrical plan it has the trim, neat appearance of a toy cathedral carved out of wood and set on a green-painted square.

W H HUDSON, 1909

The classic view of the cathedral shown in 19730 (opposite top) has changed little in over a hundred years. The tranquil surface of the River Avon gently reflects the majesty of the cathedral and its incomparably magnificent 404-foot spire, the tallest in England. The famous water meadows on the right, as painted by Constable, still exist; the fields on the left are now the Queen Elizabeth Gardens.

Built in 1331, St Ann's Gate (also known as the East Gate) links the cathedral close with St John's Street and Exeter Street, and was the Vicars Choral Chapel before the cathedral choir was established (56367p, above). The room with a large window over the gate was the chapel. The close walls here were built in the 14th century using the old stone from the original cathedral at Old Sarum.

The main body of the cathedral was completed in a short span of 40 years between 1220 and 1260, in one Gothic style, Early English, so unlike most cathedrals the interior has an impressive architectural unity (19758, page 32). The light Chilmark limestone, quarried only ten miles away, contrasts with the dark Purbeck marble of the slender shafts supporting the arches. This vast cathedral church needed about 70,000 tons of stone to build it, and 28,000 tons of timber was needed for the roof. The soaring spire was completed by about 1333; today it leans somewhat. In the north nave aisle is the oldest working clock in Europe, constructed in 1386.

Salisbury Cathedral, my dear Jonas, is an edifice replete with venerable associations, and strikingly suggestive of the loftiest emotions.
CHARLES DICKENS, 'MARTIN CHUZZLEWIT'

The tradition is that in the cathedral there are 365 windows to match the number of days in a year and 8,760 pillars to match the number of hours in a year. Here in the Lady Chapel (19774, left) the slim pillars harmonise with the lancet windows, and the unusual design of the vaulted roof gives an almost light-hearted effect.

MAGNA CARTA

One of the original copies of the Magna Carta is kept in the Chapter House. Only four original copies of this important historical document survive, the best-preserved copy in Salisbury, two in the British Library in London, and one at Lincoln Cathedral. This famous 'Great Charter' was an agreement made at Runnymede between King John and his barons in 1215, which established, amongst other matters, that no free man should be imprisoned or prosecuted without fair trial – the basic principles laid out here were adopted for the constitution of the USA. The Magna Carta is beautifully written on vellum (treated calf skin). It was brought to Salisbury by William Longspee, Earl of Salisbury and half-brother to King John; Longspee was buried in the cathedral.

The chapter house (19779, opposite right), built in the mid 13th century, is one of twelve surviving medieval octagonal chapter houses, which were used as the meeting place of the cathedral clergy or the Dean and Chapter. The name 'Chapter' is thought to derive from the practice of reading a chapter of the Bible at these meetings. One of the original copies of the Magna Carta is kept in the Chapter House.

The intricate carvings in the spandrels of the wall arcade in the Chapter House (63761, above) depict fifty-five scenes from Genesis and Exodus, the last being the granting of the Commandments.

Salisbury Cathedral has the oldest surviving mechanical clock in Britain (S48711, left), built and installed in 1386. Because of its early date it is comparatively primitive: it has no face, and only strikes the hours. It once had a characteristic foliot balance and verge escapement, but this was replaced by a pendulum in the late 17th century. The clock was originally housed in the cathedral bell tower, but when this was demolished in the 18th century the clock was transferred to the central tower. A brand new clock was installed in 1884, and the old clock was stored away in the tower and only found again in 1929. In 1956 it was restored to full working order.

Opposite left: SALISBURY CATHEDRAL, THE LADY CHAPEL 1887   19774

Opposite right: SALISBURY CATHEDRAL, THE CHAPTER HOUSE 1887   19779

Above: SALISBURY CATHEDRAL, THE CHAPTER HOUSE CARVINGS 1911   63761

Left: SALISBURY CATHEDRAL, THE OLDEST CLOCK 2004   S48711

One of the peculiarities of Winchester is the amount of comparatively open land, even in the heart of the city. As we glance down upon it from the brow of St Giles' Hill, spots of foliage pleasantly interrupt the roof-lines, even where the chimneys bristle thickest; and athwart the lower part, a broad belt of gardens and groves extends from the College premises to beyond the Hospital of St John. In the middle are the cathedral precincts, and over the tops of stately limes rise its massive central tower and long line of roof. As the centre and the special glory of Winchester, we will notice this building first. It must be admitted that the exterior is at first sight rather disappointing. The sky-line is poor; the tower, massive and comparatively low, does little to relieve its monotony. Winchester has the same defect as St Alban's Abbey: one misses a central spire, as at Norwich, or a great western tower, as at Ely, or, such a pair as grace the noble facade of Durham. VICTORIAN GUIDEBOOK

From St Giles' Hill (the site of St Giles' Fair in medieval times) we look south-east over the rooftops towards the east end of Winchester's cathedral (19401, right). Nearest to us is the retrochoir with its three chapels, all built in the early 13th century (the Lady Chapel was remodelled in the 15th century). Then comes the higher roof of the chancel (we can just see the flying buttresses supporting this part of the building). On each side extend the early Norman transepts, essentially unchanged since the cathedral was built, and above is the somewhat stumpy late Norman tower.

Above: WINCHESTER CATHEDRAL 1911 63722
Right: WINCHESTER, FROM ST GILES' HILL 1886 19401

WINCHESTER CATHEDRAL

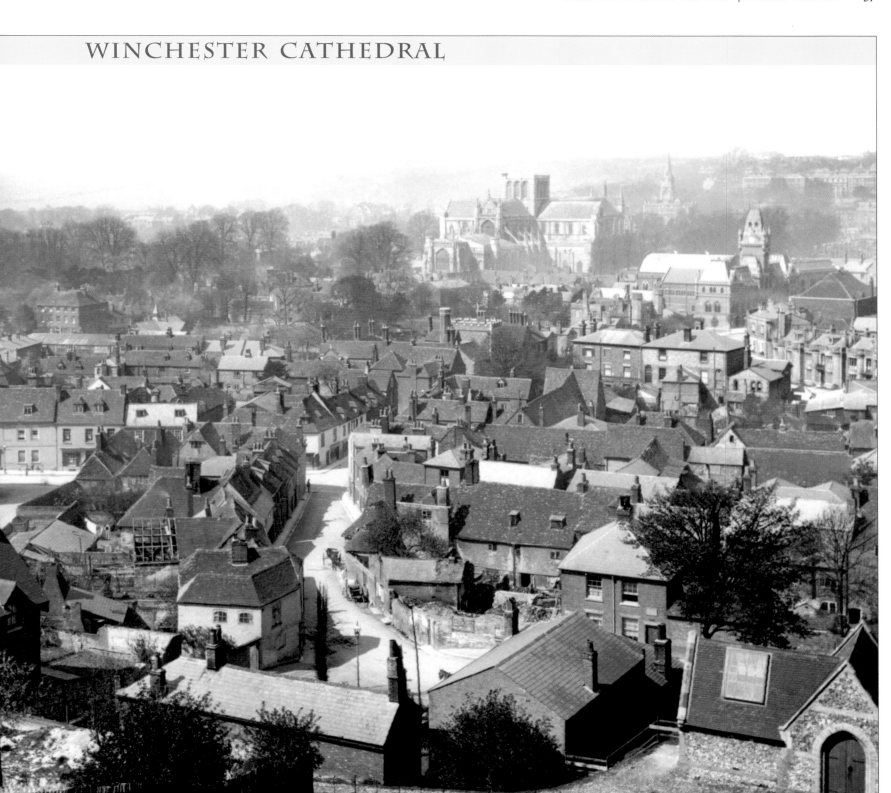

Photograph 63722 (previous page) gives us some idea of the immense length of the cathedral: at 556 feet, it is the longest Gothic church in Europe. A Saxon minster church was established here in AD643, but it was the Norman bishop Walkelin who began the cathedral we see today.

Inside the cathedral is the stunning 12th-century black marble font from Tournai in Belgium, carved with scenes from the life of St Nicholas (below, 23989). Here we see St Nicholas passing dowries to the daughters of impoverished noblemen. The other faces show birds and salamanders. There are also some magnificent 14th-century carved stalls, and older coffers containing the bones of various Saxon and Danish kings, probably including William II (William Rufus) and King Canute. During restoration work in the reign of Henry VIII the bones were re-interred in these caskets because there was no way of knowing who was who. As an old chronicler recorded: 'Not knowing which were Kings and which were bishops, because there were no inscriptions over the monuments ... Henry placed in leaden sarcophagi Kings and bishops, bishops and Kings, all mixed together.' Many other distinguished figures also lie here, among them Jane Austen and Izaak Walton.

The Chapel of the Holy Sepulchre (64454, far right) was built in the 12th century as a chapel where miracle plays were presented. On Good Friday an altar cross was transferred to the chapel and the monks re-enacted the discovery of Christ's empty tomb. The intricate painted frescoes date from the late 12th century.

Far right WINCHESTER CATHEDRAL, THE CHAPEL OF THE HOLY SEPULCHRE 1912 64454

Near right: WINCHESTER CATHEDRAL, THE FONT 1890 23989

 WINCHESTER'S HEROIC DIVER

The cathedral stands on marshy ground, and the crypt often floods. By 1905 serious subsidence to the structure had occurred: cracks appeared on the south and east walls of the cathedral, and it was feared that the whole building might collapse unless major underpinning of the foundations was carried out – the cathedral was standing on timber rafts constructed in the 11th century. A deep-sea diver, William Walker, was employed to go deep into the marshy water beneath and shore up the building. He had to work in total darkness for six hours a day in water 6 metres deep – the lonely, cold task lasted 5½ years. Walker was awarded a medal for his outstanding services, the MVO, by George V, who commented that Walker had 'saved the cathedral with his own two hands'. William Walker died during the influenza epidemic of 1918, but his extraordinary achievement will always be remembered. Today, a bronze statue commemorates the brave man who saved the cathedral.

NETLEY ABBEY

The ferryman who rowed me, a lusty young Fellow, told me, that he would not for all the world pass a night at the Abbey, (there were such things seen near it,) tho' there was a power of money hid there.

THOMAS GRAY, 1764

Above: NETLEY ABBEY 1908   60467

Below: NETLEY ABBEY 1908   60474

Founded in 1239 by the Bishop of Winchester (and after his death a year later supported by Henry III), Netley was a daughter house of Beaulieu Abbey. After the Dissolution Sir William Paulet converted the abbey into a grand mansion; the nave of the abbey church became his hall. In the 18th century the abbey passed to a Southampton builder – he was killed by falling tracery as he began to demolish the site. Part of the north transept was re-erected as a folly at Cranbury Park. Netley's church of St Edward the Confessor contains a medieval effigy of a crusader monk, which was found in the wall of nearby Netley Castle and probably came from Netley Abbey. However, despite all these alterations and depredations, the abbey remained remarkably complete, and the beautiful ruins are still a picturesque sight, though perhaps not quite as picturesque as they were when plants and ivy were draped over them.

Horace Walpole was awe-struck during his visit in 1755: 'The ruins are vast, and retain fragments of beautiful fretted roofs pendent in the air, with all variety of Gothic patterns of windows wrapped round and round with ivy – many trees are sprouted up among the walls, and only want to be increased with cypresses! … In short, they are not the ruins of Netley, but of paradise …'

ROMSEY ABBEY

R omsey Abbey is said to be the only Norman nunnery church still standing in England. After being in existence for 600 years, the Benedictine nunnery was closed in 1539. By then only a few nuns remained, and the Crown took the nunnery's possessions. The church was spared, since the people of Romsey were using it as their parish church and were able to raise the huge sum of £100 demanded by Henry VIII for this most important building.

The abbey was founded by King Edward the Elder, the son and successor of King Alfred the Great, in AD907. The first-known abbess was Edward's daughter, Princess Aelflaed. From the time of its foundation the abbey drew well-born ladies as nuns, and daughters of important families were sent here to be educated. Queen Margaret of Scotland's daughters came here to be in the care of their aunt Christina, who was one of the nuns. The elder princess married Henry I in 1100, and became known as 'Good Queen Maud'. As well as the nuns and the children being educated here, there were also many servants. The abbess, who was chosen by the nuns, held a very important position. She was not only the spiritual leader: she had secular responsibilities too, both in the town and relating to the abbey's property. The wealth and importance of the abbey is shown by its great length of 263 feet and its proportionate width. Timber, land and estates were granted to the abbey, and a steward was employed to manage its properties, which were scattered over Hampshire and beyond. In the 14th century there were about 100 nuns, most of whom brought dowries. The Black Death in the mid 14th century, which drastically lowered the whole population of the country, badly affected the abbey. Many nuns died, and their numbers never exceeded 25 in later years.

Left: ROMSEY ABBEY, THE NAVE LOOKING EAST 1904   51433

Above: ROMSEY ABBEY FROM GREENHILL 1903 49326

Right: ROMSEY ABBEY, THE NORTH AISLE 1904 51435

THE EDUCATIONAL WORK OF NUNNERIES

All the larger nunneries and probably most of the smaller ones, opened their doors for the education of young girls, who were frequently boarders. In fact the female portion of the population, the poor as well as the rich, had in the convents their only schools, nuns their only teachers, in pre-Reformation times.

John Aubrey writes as an eye-witness of the Wiltshire convents that 'the young maids were brought up ... at nunneries, where they had examples of piety, and humility, and modesty, and obedience to imitate and to practise. Here they learned needlework, the art of confectionery, surgery (for anciently there were no apothecaries or surgeons - the gentlewomen did cure their poor neighbours: their hands are now too fine), physic, writing, drawing, etc. Old Jacques could see from his house the nuns of the priory (St Mary's, near Kington St Michael) come forth into the nymph-hay with their rocks and wheels to spin: and with their sewing work. He would say that he had told threescore and ten: but of nuns there were not so many, but in all, with lay sisters and widows, old maids and young girls, there might be such a number. This,' he concludes, 'was a fine way of breeding up young women, who are led more by example than precept; and a good retirement for widows and grave single women to a civil, virtuous, and holy life.'

BEAULIEU ABBEY

Beaulieu – the name is Norman-French, and means 'beautiful place' – was founded as a Cistercian abbey by King John in 1204; most of the buildings were 13th-century, except the gatehouse, which was rebuilt in the 14th century (and converted into a house in the 19th century, now the main part of the present-day mansion). The abbey was purchased by Thomas Wriothesley, 1st Earl of Southampton, at its dissolution in 1538. The abbey church and most of the buildings went to ruin (the stone was used to build Henry VIII's coastal castles), except for the refectory (to the right in photograph 60484), which the parish took over as the parish church, an almost certainly unique arrangement. One rare treasure here is the old pulpit from which readings were given to the monks at meal times. This photograph looks across the cloister to the three arches which once led to the chapter house. The Domus, which once housed the lay brothers' refectory, now contains an exhibition of monastic life in a series of modern embroidered wall hangings.

Left: BEAULIEU ABBEY 1908 60484

CHICHESTER CATHEDRAL

Above: CHICHESTER CATHEDRAL FROM THE CANAL 1898   42684

In this dense and various old England two places may be very near together and yet strike a very different note. I knew in a general way that [Chichester] had for its main sign a cathedral, and indeed had caught the sign, in the form of a beautiful spire, from the window of the train. I had always regarded an afternoon in a small cathedral-town as a high order of entertainment, and a morning at Portsmouth had left me in the mood for not missing such an exhibition. The spire of Chichester at a little distance greatly resembles that of Salisbury. It is on a smaller scale, but it tapers upward with a delicate slimness which, like that of its famous rival, makes a picture of the level landscape in which it stands. Unlike the spire of Salisbury, however, it has not at present the charm of antiquity. A few years ago the old steeple collapsed and tumbled into the church, and the present structure is but a modern facsimile …

HENRY JAMES, 1879

The piers of the tower were found to be rotten. There was no adhesion in the core. Every effort was made to renew the piers, but every effort was useless. A heavy gale on the night of Wednesday, February 20th, 1861, precipitated the calamity; and on the next day, at about twenty minutes past one in the afternoon, the writer saw the spire move gently and bodily towards the south-west, then it seemed to recover itself, and spire and tower sank out of sight, with little noise, into the centre of the building. With the exception of the capstone, which fell upon one of the flying buttresses of the nave, every stone fell within the church. The weather-cock alone was picked up in the churchyard, and a heap of disintegrated materials filled the cross of the church up to the level of the triforium. We need not describe the rebuilding. The work was placed under the care of the late Sir Gilbert Scott, and it never ceased until the church was reopened in November, 1867.

C A SWAINSON, 1884

Left: CHICHESTER CATHEDRAL, FROM THE NORTH EAST 1892   29984

Opposite above: CHICHESTER CATHEDRAL, THE CLOISTERS AND ST RICHARD'S PORCH 1892 29995

Ralph Luffa, Bishop from 1091 to 1123, was responsible for building the bulk of Chichester's cathedral, a splendid Norman building, with the west part of the nave completed by Seffrid I in the 1130s. The cathedral had a disastrous fire in 1187 which led to a new east end and much re-facing; also, stone vaults were added throughout. Two towers were blown down in 1210, and the rebuilt central tower received a 271-foot spire around 1300. The spire and tower collapsed in 1861; when the spire was rebuilt by Sir George Gilbert Scott he added six feet to its height. There was an old rhyme whose prophecy was fulfilled by the tower falling: 'If Chichester tower do fall, in England there's no King at all.' There was indeed no King, for Queen Victoria was on the throne at the time.

Despite having a three-sided cloister, the cathedral was not a monastic foundation, so the cloisters (29995, above) serve to enclose a tranquil grassy area known as The Paradise. St Richard, whose brightly painted statue is in the niche above the double arch, was Bishop from 1245 to 1253, and was canonised by the Pope in 1262.

BOXGROVE PRIORY

Boxgrove Priory, near Chichester, was founded for Benedictine monks in about 1108. Originally there were only three monks here; numbers increased gradually to a total of nineteen monks in the mid 13th century. At the time of the Dissolution there were eight priests, one novice, twenty-eight servants and eight children living here. After the Dissolution in 1536 the parishioners moved into the monks' choir, a beautiful early 13th-century building with a vaulted roof supported by arcades of four double bays; they also retaining the crossing and a

low Norman tower, but they demolished the nave. The crossing tower of the 1170s is seen here, but the remains of the chapter house front are hidden by trees beyond the ivy-covered wall behind the girl in the straw hat (left).

At the Dissolution, most of the buildings of the priory were demolished. Today, there is little left except the three arches at the entrance to the chapter house and the ruined walls of a three-storey guest house to the north of the church, which we see here.

Top: BOXGROVE PRIORY 1899   44895P
Above: BOXGROVE PRIORY 1899   44890

The high altere, that was borne up with fower great pillars, having abowt it v chapelles ... All this is downe a Thursday and Fryday last. Now we are plucking downe a hygher vaute, borne up by fower thicke and grose pillars ... in circumference xlv fote.

THOMAS CROMWELL'S DEMOLITION AGENT

LEWES PRIORY

Above: LEWES PRIORY 1894 34509

After the battle of Hastings, William the Conqueror gave the town of Lewes and the surrounding area to one of his favourite knights, William de Warenne; he was the husband of Gundrada, who was alleged to be the daughter, or foster-daughter, of King William. In about 1077 de Warenne and Gundrada made a pilgrimage to Rome, and on the way back they stopped at a Cluniac monastery in Burgundy. They liked it so much that they decided to build a similar one in Lewes, and this, the Priory of St Pancras, became the first Cluniac establishment in England, and later the most wealthy and powerful in the country. When Henry VIII declared himself the supreme governor of the Church of England, he decided that he had the right to the priory's wealth (it had formerly belonged to the mother monastery at Cluny). In 1537 the priory was surrendered to the king, and a year later Thomas Cromwell sent an Italian engineer to destroy it. Today, only some of the walls remain, hardly enough to remind us of the extent of the original buildings. Three hundred years later, in 1845, Victorian workmen were building the Brighton to Lewes railway through the middle of the priory ruins when they unearthed two lead caskets, which contained the bones of William de Warenne and Gundrada – they now lie in the church of St John the Baptist nearby.

MICHELHAM PRIORY

The buildings of Michelham Priory are set within a large rectangular wet moat fed by the Cuckmere River, which forms the moat's north-west arm. The 'island' formed by the moat is entered over a 16th-century bridge and through a fine 15th-century Wealden sandstone gatehouse, seen here from within the moat.

Michelham Priory was founded in 1229 as a house for 13 Augustinian canons, who took over a Norman moated manor house. The priory was dissolved by Henry VIII in 1537 and the church was demolished, but much of the priory was incorporated in the Tudor mansion seen in M275311 (above). Medieval Gothic arches can be seen beyond the cedar tree's spreading boughs, while the rest of the house has more of a Tudor character.

In 1959 Mrs Stella Hotblack bought the priory and promptly gave it to the Sussex Archaeological Society, a pro-active antiquarian society that also owns Anne of Cleves House Museum in Lewes, Fishbourne Roman Palace and Lewes Castle. There are many attractions here, including a physic garden, a rope museum, and an Iron Age centre. There are several important farm buildings including the Long Barn and the monks' watermill, which has been restored and is now grinding corn again.

Above: MICHELHAM PRIORY, THE GATEHOUSE C1965 M275007

Above right: MICHELHAM PRIORY C1955 M275311

Below right: MICHELHAM PRIORY, A SUSSEX BROAD-WHEELED WAGON C1965 M275016

BATTLE ABBEY

Above: BATTLE ABBEY, THE EAST TERRACE 1910   62967

WEDNESDAY, AUGUST 20 *After breakfast we entered the abbey domains, which lay high (and that is unusual): the gateway is of gloomy authority, and the abbey commands pleasing views; but there is no care, no taste, no cleanliness! All the habitable part of the building is meanly and modernly glazed: the stables are under old arches, and above them is a prodigious grand hall in shameful rubbish, with a ruinous modern roof, falling down; and the sooner that happens the better. Underneath this building are a variety of vaults, which serve for cellarings and the holding of mortar, etc.*

JOHN BYNG, 1788, 'RIDES ROUND BRITAIN' (EDITED BY D ADAMSON, FOLIO SOCIETY)

William the Conqueror, having beaten and killed the Anglo-Saxon King Harold on Senlac Hill in 1066, vowed to found an abbey on the site of the great battle, known to history as the battle of Hastings. The small town of Battle grew up when the people who built and maintained the abbey settled there. William gave the Benedictine abbey a market which was held in front of the abbey's gates, although the present magnificent gatehouse was built for Abbot Alan of Ketling in 1338 to replace the Norman one. At its dissolution in 1538 the abbey was given to Sir Anthony Browne, a great friend of Henry VIII, who demolished the abbey church and the cloisters and turned the remaining buildings into a grand residence. The building is now in the care of English Heritage, and leased to Battle Abbey School.

The abbot's Great Hall (62981, above) is the centrepiece of the remaining abbey buildings. Originally of the 15th century, it has now been made more medieval than it was: the minstrels' gallery and the massive fireplace were added in the 1850s by Henry Clutton.

Above: BATTLE ABBEY, THE ABBOT'S HALL 1910   62981

Right: BATTLE ABBEY, THE GATEHOUSE 1927   80411P

CANTERBURY CATHEDRAL

In this mid-Victorian view (above), Canterbury Cathedral is very much the tallest building in the city. The wonderful clustering of the richly-surfaced and pinnacled Gothic towers rise from the transepts and elements of the nave of Archbishop Lanfranc's first Norman cathedral. The earlier cathedral had conveniently burnt down in 1067, and Lanfranc set about rebuilding it as soon as he became archbishop in 1070. Canterbury Cathedral has been an object of pilgrimage for very many centuries, a pilgrimage immortalised by Geoffrey Chaucer in his 'Canterbury Tales', which depicts a group of pilgrims setting out from Southwark to Canterbury. The object of their journey was the shrine of St Thomas à Becket, the Archbishop of Canterbury famously martyred in 1170 by four of Henry II's over-zealous knights (see a drawing of his monument on page 53). The cult of St Thomas meant that Canterbury rapidly became the focus of one of three major European pilgrimages; the other two were Santiago de Compostela in western Spain, and, of course, the mother church of all western Christendom in the Middle Ages, Rome.

Beneath the ivy in 25685 (opposite left) is Prior Sellyng's Gatehouse, built between 1472 and 1494, which separated the monks' world from the great north court surrounded by service buildings, such as the bakehouse, brewery, granary and kitchens, the lodgings, and pilgrims' accommodation.

Above: CANTERBURY CATHEDRAL C1875   12053

Opposite left: CANTERBURY CATHEDRAL, THE NORTH GATE 1890   25685

Opposite right: CANTERBURY CATHEDRAL, THE NAVE LOOKING EAST 1888   21366

THE NAVE

Somewhat cold, somewhat unearthly almost, is the impression made by the forest of pillars rising through the clerestory to the vaulted roof; stretching away to the central tower – Bell Harry – where light shines down into the gloom. A beautiful place wherein to rest and dream dreams of the past. All now is grey, but in bygone ages the great church blazed with colours; paintings and rich hangings adorned the walls; there were numberless altars with their tiny points of light, and all was enriched and at the same time mellowed by the splendour shed upon pavement and pillar from the 'storied windows richly dight'.

W TEIGNMOUTH SHORE, 1907

In 1378 Prior Hathbrand had Lanfranc's nave demolished, except for the north-west tower, the north aisle wall and the crossing tower; the demolition was paid for by Archbishop Sudbury, who was to be killed during the Peasants' Revolt in 1381. Little building took place until 1391, so pilgrims must have seen a curiously truncated cathedral. Prior Chillenden, an indefatigable builder and an improving prior, employed Henry Yevele to design and supervise the new nave, which was completed in 1405. This photograph (21366, above) shows the view inside Yevele's rebuilt nave. It shows the piers as a cluster of shafts and colonettes, with very little of the arches visible in long views. Presumably this effect was intended, but one can see Yevele scratching his head at being forced to follow the narrow bay widths of Lanfranc's nave.

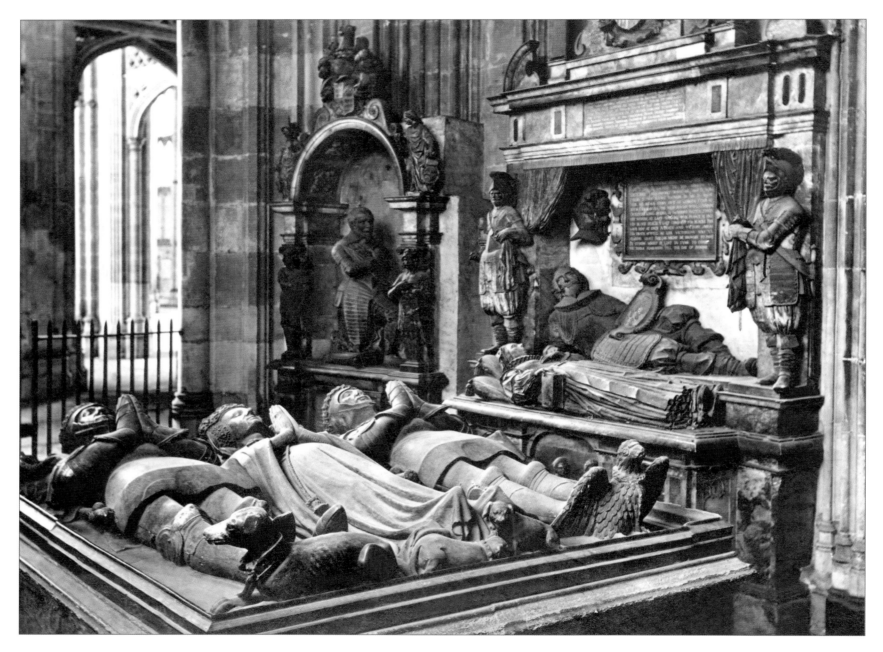

St Michael's Chapel in the south transept was built for Lady Margaret Holland, daughter of the Earl of Kent. It has a splendidly intricate stone lierne vault, and it is stuffed with superb monuments. Also known as the Warriors' Chapel, it is now the Chapel of the Royal East Kent Regiment, and is hung with their battle flags. In pride of place in the centre of the chapel is the tomb chest of Lady Margaret Holland, who died a few days after the chapel was dedicated in May 1439. She lies between her two coroneted husbands, John Beaufort, Earl of Somerset and son of John of Gaunt, and Thomas, Duke of Clarence, the second son of Henry IV. She married well, and both husbands pre-deceased her. At the foot of the tomb of Lady Holland and her two husbands is the tomb slab of the important Archbishop Stephen Langton, who died in 1228; he was instrumental in forcing King John to sign the Magna Carta in 1215. It is suggested that Lady Holland was influential enough to get his monument slid into a special recess in the wall to make way for her tomb chest, although others think the tomb was in the churchyard beyond the Norman apse that the chapel replaced and that the wall was arched over it.

I made my way down into the crypt, which is a magnificent maze of low, dark arches and pillars, and groped about till I found the place where the frightened monks had first shuffled the inanimate victim of Moreville and Fitzurse out of the reach of further desecration. While I stood there a violent thunderstorm broke over the cathedral; great rumbling gusts and rain-drifts came sweeping through the open sides of the crypt and, mingling with the darkness which seemed to deepen and flash in corners and with the potent mouldy smell, made me feel as if I had descended into the very bowels of history.

HENRY JAMES, 1877

This view (right) looks towards the Trinity Choir south aisle, showing the paired and elegantly-proportioned arcade columns with their richly carved foliage capitals. The round-topped rendered brick tomb chest is that of the exiled French cardinal, Odo Coligny, murdered by a treacherous servant who gave him a poisoned apple! Although a cardinal, he had Huguenot leanings; he was given asylum by Queen Elizabeth I in 1568, having fled from France, which was then in the grip of the Wars of Religion.

Opposite: CANTERBURY CATHEDRAL, ST MICHAEL'S CHAPEL C1862 1087
Above left: CANTERBURY CATHEDRAL, THE CRYPT 1898 40844
Above: CANTERBURY CATHEDRAL, THE MONUMENT TO BECKET
Left: CANTERBURY CATHEDRAL, TRINITY CHAPEL C1862 1085

MEDIEVAL BUILDING STYLES

In the early Middle Ages, churches and cathedrals were built in the Romanesque style: thick walls, sturdy round arches and massive pillars were needed to bear the weight of the barrel roofs. Mouldings were plain, pillar capitals were cushion-shape or scalloped, and windows and arches were often decorated with zig-zag carving. By the 12th century, the Gothic style was developed: slim pillars supported the stone ribs of the vaulted roofs, which formed pointed arches; this strong yet light framework enabled the building to be higher than before. The weight of the roof was supported by external buttresses, often flying buttresses, thus allowing the walls to be thinner and the windows larger. Over the centuries, roof vaulting grew ever more complex, culminating in the glorious fan vaulting of the Perpendicular period; and from the tall, narrow Early English lancets, windows grew larger and larger, to be filled with glowing stained glass.

DAVINGTON PRIORY

Davington priory, and what is left of the priory church, has an ancient history. Two nuns from here were shipwrecked at Reculver on their way to Minster-in-Thanet. To give thanks for the saving of their lives, they instituted the construction of the twin church towers that once existed at Davington. Thereafter the Reculver towers were called 'the two sisters'. What was left of the priory was severely damaged in 1781 when a Faversham gunpowder mill exploded. Since then the priory has undergone extensive restoration, and is now a private house.

Left: DAVINGTON PRIORY 1892   31479

TENTERDEN ST BENEDICT'S PRIORY

In 1867, during the time of the Roman Catholic revival in the 19th century, the Benedictine fathers of an Anglo-Belgian congregation from Ramsgate established a priory at Finchden on the Appledore Road. This was the first known time that Mass had been celebrated in Tenterden since the Reformation. The chapel was opened to the public, a school was started, and many baptisms took place over the next ten years. The priory was closed in 1877, and the community was transferred to Canterbury. The priory has since reverted to its original name of Finchden.

Right: TENTERDEN, ST BENEDICT'S PRIORY 1903 44999

THE MEDIEVAL MASON

The stonemasons of medieval times were highly skilled craftsmen. The master mason had overall charge of a building project. Using only compasses, set square and a measuring rod, thanks to his knowledge of geometry and experience of engineering, he was able to plan some of the most astonishing structures ever built. The masons who worked under him (and the carpenters and glaziers) were skilled tradesmen who had their apprentices working with them. The building work was hard and dangerous; as the walls rose, masons had to work at a great height on flimsy scaffolding lashed together with rope. Stones were carved on the ground, and then lifted by cranes and pulleys in baskets (or with a device called a lewis – its legs fit into a slot in the stone, and the lifting rope goes through its shackle) to be set in place. Arches in arcades, windows and flying buttresses were formed round wooden supports called centering. Construction work was done in the spring and summer, allowing the mortar to set and the building to settle during the winter, and giving the masons time to carve the stones.

Above: ROCHESTER, THE CASTLE AND THE CATHEDRAL 1894 34029P

Above right: DRAWING OF ROCHESTER CATHEDRAL, WEST DOOR

Below right: ROCHESTER CATHEDRAL, THE CRYPT C1955 R44153

Opposite: ROCHESTER CATHEDRAL 1894 34012

ROCHESTER CATHEDRAL

This cathedral is the legacy of Bishop Gundulf, who not only began the process of castle building at Rochester, but also started to replace the 400-year-old cathedral he had inherited. Beginning with a square tower in the 1070s (Gundulf's Tower), the present cathedral slowly evolved for the benefit of the laity of Rochester and for the community of Benedictine monks who settled there during the Norman period. Cathedral construction was a very lengthy process, and the building's final appearance includes various styles which went in and out of fashion during the occupation of the Rochester diocese by Bishop Gundulf's successors. Many of the cathedral's Gothic features were financed with donations given by pilgrims visiting the shrine of William of Perth. This Scottish baker had been on his way to the Holy Land when he was murdered near Rochester in 1201. He was venerated after miracles were attributed to him.

The Norman west front of England's second oldest cathedral after Canterbury is one of the best of its kind, with a finely sculpted main doorway. The large window was inserted in the 15th century, and the Victorians restored it as a memorial to those Royal Engineers who died in the Afghan and South African wars. In this photograph (34012, above), the building had quite recently been rescued from near ruin with a restoration that included the removal of the spire in 1823 and the addition of the tower pinnacles.

Beneath the choir transept lies the beautifully vaulted crypt (R44153, opposite below). Two Norman bays remain from the time the cathedral was first built.

Externally the cathedral cannot be called an impressive building. Small in itself, there is nothing in its outline to enhance its dimensions or appeal to the senses by grace of outline instead of grandeur of size. It is without western towers; and the central one is low and squat; at a glance it proclaims itself modern or modernised, and is no better, perhaps worse, than most Gothic of the early Victorian period. We pass from the High Street of Rochester beneath one of the old gateways of the monastery, now almost buried in houses, through a comparatively narrow passage into the precincts of the cathedral. The view, however, of its western part is impeded by the Church of St. Nicholas, which stands immediately to the south of the western part of the nave, and after passing this we reach the little open space in front of the main entrance. Here, if we are readers of Dickens, we may remember how he has interwoven the main features of the scene with the story of his last and unfinished work, and if it be summer-time, through the open west door of the cathedral we may look 'down the throat of old time'.

T G BONNEY, 1884

LONDON, ST PAUL'S CATHEDRAL

Perched on the summit of Ludgate Hill at the highest point in the city, St Paul's Cathedral, Sir Christopher Wren's masterpiece and one of the greatest buildings in the world, is the pride of London. It took about ten years to design St Paul's and 40 years to build it. In 1666, just before the Great Fire, Wren had recommended that the unstable tower of Old St Paul's, the vast medieval cathedral, should be replaced by a dome. However, the Great Fire reduced Old St Paul's to a virtual ruin, and in 1668 Wren was commissioned to design a new cathedral. His First Model, a design to be built on the old foundations, was quickly rejected, and in the 1670s he produced his Greek Cross design and then his Great Model, remarkable both for its espousal of the Renaissance style rather than Gothic and for its plan – the main space was set beneath a huge central dome. But this plan was too revolutionary for the clergy, so in 1674–75 Wren reluctantly produced a more traditional aisled, longitudinal plan (the Warrant Design), with a smaller dome topped by a spire. However, as building work went on, Wren was able to regain many of the elements of the Great Model – Wren's son recounts how King Charles II 'was pleas'd to allow him the liberty in the Prosecution of his work, to make some variations … as from Time to Time he should see proper'.

Many great men and women are buried in St Paul's, including Wren himself; on his grave is inscribed: 'Si monumentum requiris, circumspice' – 'If you want to see a monument to him, look around you'. The Duke of Wellington's imposing monument is here, and so is Nelson's. Others buried here include the playwright James Barrie, and the painters Sir Joshua Reynolds, Opie, Turner, Millais, and Landseer.

St Paul's was finally completed in 1711, and throughout the building process Wren continued to modify the design. The huge dome familiar to us today was built, not a smaller dome and spire. The longitudinal elements of the Warrant Design were altered, so that there was after all a central space beneath the dome. 'At first', says the late Victorian writer A R Hope Moncrieff, 'the effect of the interior must have been rather austere, and it was long before cold Georgian piety ceased to be suspicious of decoration'. Of course, he was writing in an era when opulent decoration and rich colour were the height of fashion; today, when many of us favour minimalism, the 'cold' Georgian style is more to our taste. What Hope Moncrieff calls 'this nobly massive structure' is indeed a national treasure.

Opposite: LONDON, THE WATER-FRONT BY ST PAUL'S 1890 L130017

Above left: LONDON, ST PAUL'S CATHEDRAL, THE CHOIR, LOOKING EAST C1890 L130235

Above right: LONDON, ST PAUL'S CATHEDRAL, THE CRYPT CHAPEL C1890 L130134

Right: LONDON, ST PAUL'S CATHEDRAL, DRAWING OF THE WELLINGTON MONUMENT

OXFORD, CHRIST CHURCH

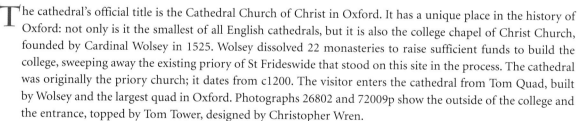

The cathedral's official title is the Cathedral Church of Christ in Oxford. It has a unique place in the history of Oxford: not only is it the smallest of all English cathedrals, but it is also the college chapel of Christ Church, founded by Cardinal Wolsey in 1525. Wolsey dissolved 22 monasteries to raise sufficient funds to build the college, sweeping away the existing priory of St Frideswide that stood on this site in the process. The cathedral was originally the priory church; it dates from c1200. The visitor enters the cathedral from Tom Quad, built by Wolsey and the largest quad in Oxford. Photographs 26802 and 72009p show the outside of the college and the entrance, topped by Tom Tower, designed by Christopher Wren.

In photograph 26807 (below right), we are looking east towards the chancel. The astonishing roof was built by William Orchard in about 1500. The complex ribs of the vault form star patterns, and graceful pendants of stone hang down from above. The oldest monument in the cathedral is the shrine of St Frideswide, the patron saint of Oxford; her relics were contained within it, and pilgrims came from far and wide to pray at her shrine. It was built in 1289, destroyed at the Reformation, and rebuilt in 1889.

Above: OXFORD, FROM MAGDALENE TOWER 1890   26802

Right: OXFORD, CHRIST CHURCH CATHEDRAL, THE NAVE 1890   26807

Opposite: OXFORD, CHRIST CHURCH CATHEDRAL 1922   72009P

Some time ago I went into a grey quadrangle, filled with gusty light and the crimson of creeper-leaves, tremulous or already in flight. A tall poplar, the favourite of the months from April to October, was pensively distributing its foliage upon the grass. There, the leaves became invisible, because of brilliant frost, and in a high attic I heard once again the laud or summons or complaint of bells. That was All Saints'; that, St Mary's; that, the Cathedral's; and that was their blended after-tone, seeming to come from the sky. Each bell had its own character or mood, sometimes constant, sometimes changing with the weather of the night. One, for example, spoke out sullenly and ceased, as if to return to musing that had been painfully interrupted. Another bell seemed to take deep joy in its frequent melodious duty – like some girl seated alone in her bower at easy toil, now and then lifting her head, and with her embroidery upon her knee, chanting joys past and present and yet to come. Once again I felt the mysterious pleasure of being in an elevated Oxford chamber at night, among cloud and star, – so that I seemed to join in the inevitable motion of the planets.

EDWARD THOMAS, (1878–1917)

A grim fraternity, passing grim lives in that sweet spot, that God had made so bright! Strange that Nature's voices all around them – the soft singing of the waters, the whisperings of the river grass, the music of the rushing wind – should not have taught them a truer meaning of life than this. They listened there, through the long days, in silence, waiting for a voice from heaven; and all day long and through the solemn night it spoke to them in myriad tones, and they heard it not.
JEROME K JEROME, 1889 (AT MEDMENHAM)

Above: MEDMENHAM ABBEY 1890   23715

MEDMENHAM ABBEY

Medmenham was never large or important; by the Dissolution its community had shrunk to the abbot and one monk. Only fragments of the 13th-century Cistercian abbey remain. The medieval arches and tower we see here are fake: the mock ruined tower was added in the 18th century, followed by the arcade – these embellishments were added to the south wing of an Elizabethan house built on the site of the east range of the cloister buildings. From 1775 to 1783 it was rented by the notorious Sir Francis Dashwood and used by the Order of St Francis of Wycombe ('the Hell-Fire Club'), who behaved like true Georgian libertines. In 1898 the house was restored for Robert Hudson, the soap king.

ST ALBANS CATHEDRAL

Top: ST ALBANS CATHEDRAL AND SOPWELL NUNNERY 1921   70482
Above: ST ALBANS CATHEDRAL 1921   70463

The Venerable Bede (AD673–AD735) tells us that not long after the 3rd-century martyrdom of Alban, the first Christian martyr in Britain, pilgrims were visiting the area that became St Albans: 'Sick folk are healed and frequent miracles take place to this day'.

The site of the martyrdom grew into a monastic community, and was then re-founded under the Benedictine rule by Offa, the Anglo-Saxon King of Mercia. Offa's foundation of AD793 gave St Albans its name and an abbey of 100 monks, and by the 12th century St Albans was the premier abbey of all England. It is not surprising that it was a prize much sought after by Henry VIII at the Dissolution. The military engineer Sir Richard Lee was awarded the task of realising the potential of the abbey site and arranged the demolition and sale of much of the building, re-using some of the ancient stones and tiles for his own mansion at Sopwell (see 70482).

The citizens of St Albans bought the abbey church from Henry VIII for £400 for their own parish church. For the next 300 years, it remained a financial burden as its fabric languished. In the 19th century Sir George Gilbert Scott was commissioned to save the structure. This he did in time for its newly designated role as the cathedral church for the new diocese of St Albans in 1877.

The benefactor Edmund Beckett, Lord Grimthorpe, continued the restoration and rebuilt substantial parts of this great building. Not all agree that his work enhanced the building, but then few structures incorporate so many architectural styles. The photograph on the left (70463) shows the High Altar and the delicate work of the choir stalls and cathedra (the bishop's throne), which contrasts with the plain, sturdy Norman arches.

In the background of 70482 (above left), the cathedral soars over the rooftops. The ruins in the foreground are actually those of Sopwell House, built by Sir Richard Lee out of the stones and tiles of St Albans Abbey after the Dissolution. The nunnery was founded in 1140; at the Dissolution Sir Richard bought it, and razed it to the ground to make room for his new house.

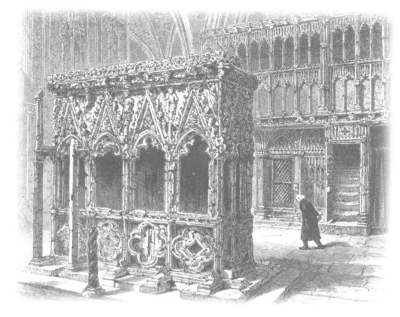

St Alban's shrine (70469, left) was destroyed at the Dissolution and was rediscovered during restoration work in the 1870s. Its foundations were all that remained; fragments from it had been used in the wall separating the Lady Chapel from the main building. The relics of the saint are long gone – Danish monks claimed to have stolen them in Saxon times, and others also claimed a part in their disappearance. The wooden watching loft was erected c1400 so that monks could supervise the visits of pilgrims in medieval times. Miraculously it survived both the Dissolution and Puritan desecration, and is unique in the country.

Left: ST ALBANS CATHEDRAL, ST ALBAN'S SHRINE AND THE WATCHING LOFT 1921 70469

Above: ST ALBANS CATHEDRAL, DRAWING OF ST ALBAN'S SHRINE

 LENTEN FOOD

The Lenten arrangements for feeding the natural man and woman from Ash Wednesday to Easter Sunday in those hardy and robust days are, even to think of, enough to turn our refined and educated stomachs. Eggs, to a certain limited extent, no doubt these good religious had; although, on the principle before explained, we do not find them mentioned, except as included in their natural producer, the domestic hen. But beyond this, during all this penitential time, the staple food, here as everywhere throughout England, was salted and dried fish.

Conger, green fish, ling, and codling stockfish, wealing or whiting, and mackerel are among those named in Russell's 'Book of Nurture' as the usual Lenten food. How tired the mouth of even the most ascetic religious must have got of the taste of salt fish, however much it was disguised with mustard sauce, or, as on great festivals, 'baken, dressed, and dished with white sugar'!

ABBOT GASQUET, 1904

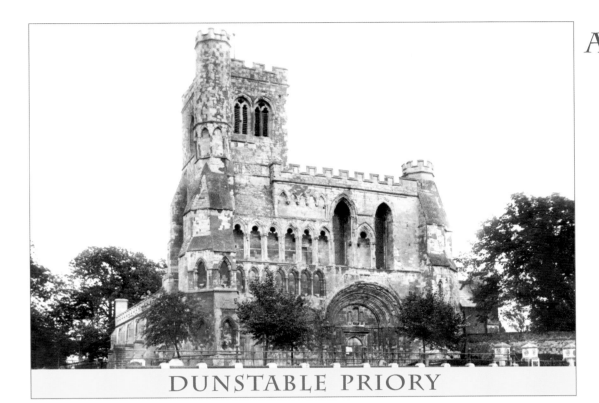

DUNSTABLE PRIORY

An Augustinian priory was established at Dunstable in 1131 by Henry I. It was at Dunstable Priory in 1533 that Archbishop Cranmer announced the official annulment of Henry VIII's marriage to Katherine of Aragon. Although the priory was closed at the Dissolution, parts of the priory church survived as the parish church of St Peter. St Peter's Church is a fine example of Norman ecclesiastical architecture, particularly the fine seven-bay nave (we see a nave aisle in 39749), and the ornate west door, which we see in 39746; the west front (39743) was restored in the Early English period after the fall of the original western towers. The existing tower was built in the 15th century as a bell tower.

Top left: DUNSTABLE, THE PRIORY CHURCH FROM THE NORTH-WEST 1897 39743

Below left: DUNSTABLE, THE PRIORY CHURCH, THE WEST DOOR 1897 39746

Above: DUNSTABLE, THE PRIORY CHURCH 1897 39749

GLOUCESTER CATHEDRAL

It will surprise many that Gloucester Cathedral has only been a cathedral since 1540 – before that it was the Benedictine abbey church of St Peter. The church was dedicated by the year 1100, and notably with the same ground plan as it has today. In 1122 the wooden roof of the central tower burst into flames during a service, and in 1170 the western tower collapsed. Helias of Hereford, a man known as a 'building enthusiast', presided over the rebuilding of the central tower in a very English style, assisted by Abbot Henry Foliot. In 1239 the church was re-dedicated by Walter Cantelupe, Bishop of Worcester. Fire again damaged the abbey in 1300. It took seven years to restore it, and Abbot John Thokey took on the challenge of building the new dormitory and the whole of the south aisle of the nave, which was ready to collapse. The windows and vaulting of the aisle stand as witness to his hard work. The cathedral boasts daring and ingenious masonry design; the fact is that the people who worked here in very dangerous conditions saved the nave from falling down like a pack of cards.

At last, I found the cathedral, though there is no point (at least, I found none) from which a very good view of the exterior can be gained. It has a very rich and beautiful outside, however, and a lofty tower, very large and ponderous, but so finished off, and adorned with pinnacles, and all manner of architectural devices – wherewith these old builders knew how to alleviate their massive structures – that it seems to sit lightly in the air. The porch was open, and some workmen were trundling barrows into the nave; so I followed, and found two young women sitting just within the porch, one of whom offered to show me round the cathedral. There was a great dust in the nave, arising from the operations of the workmen. They had been laying a new pavement, I believe, and scraping away the plaster which had heretofore been laid over the pillars and walls. The pillars come out from this process as good as new; great, round, massive columns, not clustered like those of most cathedrals … The dust and racket of the work-people quite destroyed the effect which should have been produced by the aisles and arches; so that I hardly stopped to glance at this part of the cathedral, though I saw some mural monuments, and recumbent statues, along the walls.

NATHANIEL HAWTHORNE, 1856

Opposite: GLOUCESTER CATHEDRAL, THE APPROACH 1923   73679T

Right: GLOUCESTER CATHEDRAL, THE SOUTH PORCH 1891   28972

Here we see the south porch, displaying carved figures of King Osric and Abbot Serlo on either side of the entrance. Across the top of the doorway are the six figures representing St Peter, St Paul and the four evangelists, which were carved by J F Redfern.

Gloucester is the birthplace of the Perpendicular style. Thokey and his successors all contributed to the Perpendicular parts of the church, and Abbot Wigmore, Abbot Staunton and Abbot Horton continued the vision of Thokey. The Perpendicular roof vaulting is believed to have been begun by Wigmore and his master builders in about 1350, and the work is unparalleled.

The cathedral now had a Norman nave and Gothic vaulting, and a Perpendicular choir and transepts, in a Romanesque outer shell. Thomas Seabroke planned the cathedral's greatest feature, the central tower, and Abbot Hanley and Abbot Farley finished the building off with the Lady Chapel, which left the cathedral as we know it today. The building is not a mis-match of styles and ideas, but rather has been transformed over the centuries to make a harmonious whole.

William Froucester, a renowned figure in the history of the building, completed the cloisters after 1381. Abbot Horton had started the work, and John Boyfield carried it on. It is one of the most perfect structures of its kind in existence. Imagine the monks as they retired to meditate in this area after dinner until evensong. In recent years the cloisters of Gloucester Cathedral have featured as part of Hogwarts in the 'Harry Potter' films.

Left: GLOUCESTER CATHEDRAL, THE CLOISTERS 1891   28997

CLOISTERS

We who see the cold damp-stained cloisters of the old monastic buildings as they are to-day, as at Westminster for example, may well feel a difficulty in realising what they were in the time of their glory. Day after day for centuries the cloister was the centre of the activity of the religious establishment. The quadrangle was the place where the monks lived and studied and wrote. In the three sides – the northern, eastern, and western walks – were transacted the chief business of the house, other than what was merely external. Here the older monks laboured at the tasks appointed them by obedience, or discussed questions relating to ecclesiastical learning or regular observance, or at permitted times joined in recreative conversation. Here, too, in the parts set aside for the purpose, the younger members toiled at their studies under the eye of their teacher, learnt the monastic observance from the lips of the novice-master, or practised the chants and melodies of the Divine Office with the cantor or his assistant. How the work was done in the winter time, even supposing that the great windows looking out on to the cloister-garth were glazed or closed with wooden shutters, must ever remain a mystery. In some places, it is true, certain screenwork divisions appear to have been devised, so as to afford some shelter and protection to the elder members and scribes of the monastery from the sharper draughts inevitable in an open cloister.

ABBOT GASQUET, 1904

CRANHAM, PRINKNASH ABBEY

Above:
CRANHAM,
PRINKNASH ABBEY
c1965 C179031

Left:
CRANHAM,
PRINKNASH,
THE FOUNDATIONS OF
THE NEW ABBEY c1960
C179016

Prinknash (pronounced Prinnage) Abbey is for the most part a very modern building, rising stark above the valley, but the oldest part of Prinknash Abbey dates from the 14th century – it was a grange of the Abbots of Gloucester. The old manor house dates back to the 16th century. The present Benedictine community arrived here from Caldey Island in 1928, and established a world-famous pottery – it was later sold off to a private firm, and closed in recent years. Prinknash Abbey is now an important incense blender, producing five blends based on traditional recipes that are sold all over the world: Abbey, Basilica, Cathedral, Sanctuary and Priory.

In the 1930s, Abbot Upson dreamed of a new abbey to be built a mile from the old one on a sloping site with a superb view. The abbey church was to be vast, almost as big as Gloucester Cathedral. The architect Goodhart-Rendel drew up plans; because of the steepness of the site, the church was to have a double crypt, and work on the lower storey started in 1939, as we see here. However, it later transpired that the ambitious scheme could never be completed. It was eventually decided that a smaller church would occupy the lower crypt, and in the 1960s and early 1970s the rest of the abbey was built above it. When it was completed, the uncompromisingly modern abbey was at the centre of controversy: it was hailed by some as a fine example of functional architecture, and criticised by others as stark and featureless. A great deal of the building work was done by the monks themselves.

HEREFORD CATHEDRAL

In this church there is much to admire, a good deal to learn, much to deplore.

A W PUGIN

The earliest stone church on this site dates from the 11th century, but there must have been a church here 400 years before that, because the first bishop is recorded in AD676, a man named Putta. Hereford's cathedral church is dedicated to St Mary the Virgin and St Ethelbert the King. There is a lovely medieval tradition that still survives at Hereford: the inauguration on St Nicholas's Day, 6 December, of a Boy Bishop from then until the coming Christmas. St Nicholas is the patron saint of children.

The original medieval west front of the cathedral collapsed along with its tower on Easter Monday 1786, bringing down much of the nave with it. In photograph 51915a (right) we see the west front after it had been totally remodelled. The rebuilding was finished in 1908; the work had taken several years to complete, at a cost of £15,550 16s 4d.

The font (opposite, far right) is probably the oldest object in the cathedral, dating from the 11th or 12th century; it would have been carved by master craftsmen working for what is now described as the Hereford school of carving. The carved figures represent the Apostles.

The chained library in Hereford Cathedral is the finest in the world, containing books and manuscripts that date back a thousand years or more (opposite, near right). Chaining the books kept them secure; it was possible for people to read the precious books on the ledge below, while ensuring that they could not be taken away. One of Hereford Cathedral's greatest treasures is the Mappa Mundi, a map of the world drawn by Richard of Haldingham, a monk who came from Lincolnshire. The world as it was envisioned in the Middle Ages was a strange place, inhabited by many fantastic creatures. Richard's world was flat, with Jerusalem at its centre, the British Isles strangely elongated, and Africa labelled Europe and vice versa.

Above: HEREFORD CATHEDRAL, THE WEST FRONT C1910 51915A

ST ETHELBERT

In AD794 the Mercian King Offa visited the area, accompanied by his wife and daughter, Alfthrytha, staying at Sutton Walls just north of Hereford. While they were there they received a visitor, King Ethelbert of East Anglia, who arrived as a suitor for Alfthrytha. But instead of being welcomed, King Ethelbert was brutally murdered; some say that he was killed by the jealous wife of King Offa, but in all probability it was on the orders of Offa himself. Ethelbert's body was decapitated and thrown in a ditch. But then miracles began. A light shone out from the body so that it was found. It was put on a cart to be taken to Hereford for burial, but as the cart trundled along, Ethelbert's head fell off unnoticed. A blind man walking along the road tripped over it and miraculously had his sight restored; he picked up the head and took it to Hereford. Other miracles followed, and people visiting Ethelbert's tomb were cured of all manner of ills. Ethelbert quickly became venerated as a saint. His cult was to play an important part in the development of the cathedral, drawing pilgrims from far and wide.

On approaching the cathedral excellent views of the exterior may be obtained from the well-kept close, especially from the north-east corner … The eastern gables of the choir and Lady Chapel were rebuilt from designs by Mr Cottingham (1841–1850), while the greater part of all other restoration has been earned out by the late Sir G G Scott (1856–1877). The ancient spire – wood covered with lead – was taken down in 1797. The western front, with the clerestory of the nave, was constructed in a most debased style by the architect Wyatt, who also shortened the nave by one entire bay. These works were undertaken in consequence of the disastrous fall, on Easter Monday, 1786, of the west end, whereby half the nave and a western tower were destroyed.

FRANCIS T HAVERGAL, 1884

Above: HEREFORD, DRAWING OF THE CATHEDRAL AND THE WYE BRIDGE

Near right: HEREFORD CATHEDRAL, THE CHAINED LIBRARY 1925 77352

Far right: HEREFORD CATHEDRAL, THE FONT C1869 4849

GREAT MALVERN PRIORY

At the time of the Domesday Book (1086) this part of Worcestershire was described as 'a wilderness', with 'numerous and vast thickets'. Great Malvern grew up around a Benedictine priory said to have been founded by St Wrest, who found sanctuary here from marauding Danes. The priory, which housed 30 monks, stood on land belonging to Westminster Abbey. In this photograph, we are looking at the east end of the priory church with its magnificent window; this part of the building, and the tower, date from the second half of the 15th century.

From the outside, it would seem that the priory church is entirely of the 15th century (opposite, above); but inside the nave arcades of the original building remain, the plain, dignified Norman arches springing from sturdy pillars. The priory was dissolved by Henry VIII but, fortunately for posterity, the priory church was bought by the townspeople for the sum of £20 to replace their old parish church. This does not seem a huge sum to us today, but it took the 105 families in the parish two years to raise the money. Because of a general lack of money in the parish, hardly any repairs were carried out for the next 200 years – a blessing in disguise, since it meant that many medieval features still remain here today, including the glass.

Only the priory's church and gatehouse remain (opposite, below); the rest of the buildings were taken down in the aftermath of the Dissolution. Thomas Cromwell, the architect of this destruction, was charitable to the occupants, giving pensions to the prior and the eleven remaining monks.

St Benedict formulated his Benedictine rule for religious communities in Italy at the end of the 5th century; he called it 'a very little rule for beginners', and rejected the strict asceticism of the early hermits – he hoped that his rule would establish 'nothing harsh, nothing heavy'. The Benedictine motto was moderation in all things and the importance of the community, despite the stringent requirements of poverty, chastity and obedience. The  *Cluniacs, a Benedictine order, were founded in Cluny in AD910. Two rather more austere orders were the Cistercians, founded in Citeaux in the 12th century (known as White Monks because of their white robes), and the Carthusians, founded by St Bruno at La Grande Chartreuse in 1086. Carthusian monks led fasting, solitary lives in separate cells, meeting only for services. The early 12th century saw the rise of orders of canons, who combined community life with service to parish and cathedral. They included the Augustinian, or Black Canons (named after St Augustine of Hippo), the Premonstratensian, or White Canons, and the Gilbertines, who lived in double monasteries with nuns. The orders of preaching friars, who ministered to the poor, included the Dominicans (Black Friars), Franciscans (Grey Friars), Carmelites (White Friars) and Austin Friars. Some of these orders also included nuns. The Knights Hospitallers and the Knights Templars were founded to give assistance to pilgrims to the Holy Land, to protect the holy places, and to care for the sick.*

Opposite: GREAT MALVERN, THE PRIORY CHURCH C1871   6972

Top: GREAT MALVERN, THE PRIORY CHURCH FROM THE SOUTH-EAST 1893   32389

Above: GREAT MALVERN, THE ABBEY GATE 1893   32394

WORCESTER CATHEDRAL

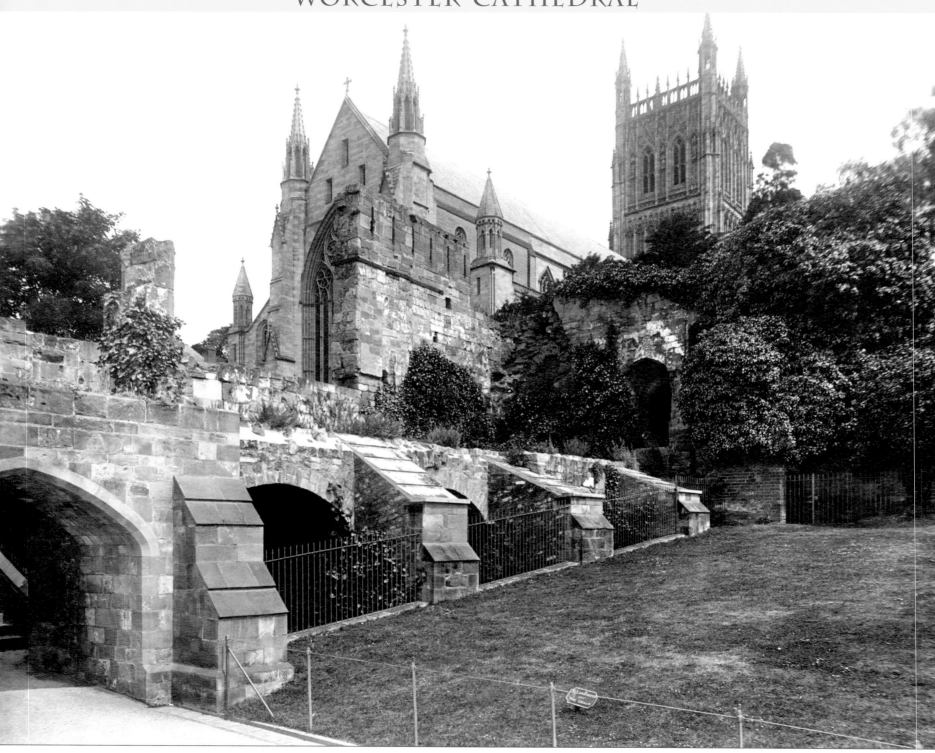

Seen from the Shrub Hill, the cathedral rises nobly against the wavy outline of the Malvern Hills; and on a bright evening in spring or autumn the level rays of the setting sun light up the windows of it across the Severn with a blaze of glory, as if it were illuminated within for some high festival … The cathedral has passed through many perils from Danish pirates and Welsh marauders, as well as from the conflagrations so frequent in the Middle Ages, and from civil wars. In 1292 – probably not then only – two rival processions fought in the cathedral. In 1641 Essex stabled his troopers, it is said, in the nave, exasperated by discovering arms hidden in the precincts. During the siege which took place in 1646 a field-piece was slung up to the top of the tower; and subsequently the lead off the roof was sold, with much else, by auction.

I GREGORY SMITH, 1884

Opposite: WORCESTER CATHEDRAL AND THE MONASTIC RUINS 1892   29884

Above: WORCESTER CATHEDRAL, THE PULPIT 1893   32095

Below: WORCESTER CATHEDRAL, THE CRYPT 1893   32101

Bishop Wulfstan of Worcester was the only Anglo-Saxon bishop not to be replaced by a Norman at the Conquest, for his great leadership abilities had been shown when he instigated the regeneration of the cathedral after its destruction by the Danes – the first cathedral had been built in the 7th century, and St Oswald had built a priory here in the 10th century. The new cathedral was begun in 1084, but the exterior is largely the result of 13th- and 14th-century rebuilding and 19th-century restoration. The original tower collapsed in 1175, and its replacement was not completed until 1374. The cathedral contains the tomb of King John (1167–1216), the first post-Conquest monarch to be buried in England; he lies at Worcester at his own request. In 1218 the remains of Worcester's two saints, Wulfstan and Oswald, were transferred from their original tombs to a shrine in the quire and King John was buried between them – they are represented by two small figures on either side of his shoulders. The monastic ruins to the left of photograph 29884 (page 74) stand between the cathedral and the River Severn, and are those of the monks' reredorter, or lavatories, conveniently sited to enable the drains to discharge straight into the river.

The earliest surviving structure in Worcester, the largest Norman crypt in England, is all that remains of St Wulfstan's cathedral of 1084 (32101, previous page). Built partly of reused masonry from St Oswald's Benedictine priory, it is very beautiful, with a forest of stone columns supporting a simple vaulted roof.

Red marble lions (one is just visible) guard the steps which rise to the ornate pulpit, carved from red, green and cream marble (32095, previous page). Designed by Sir George Gilbert Scott and made by William Forsyth, this is Victorian art at its most florid. It stands in the nave: there is a restrained and elegant 17th-century pulpit in the chancel.

The Dean's chapel in the south quire transept has a 13th-century frieze of carvings in the spandrels of the arcading (that is, between the tops of the adjoining arches). Those on the south wall feature scenes from Judgement Day, including these three members of the faithful pushing up their coffin lids as they rise from the dead (59094, right).

Above: WORCESTER CATHEDRAL, THE MRS DIGBY MONUMENT BY FRANCIS CHANTREY 1891   29316

Below left: WORCESTER CATHEDRAL, MISERICORD DEPICTING SOW AND PIGS 1907   59086

Below right: WORCESTER CATHEDRAL, RISING FROM THE DEAD 1907   59094

BROMFIELD PRIORY

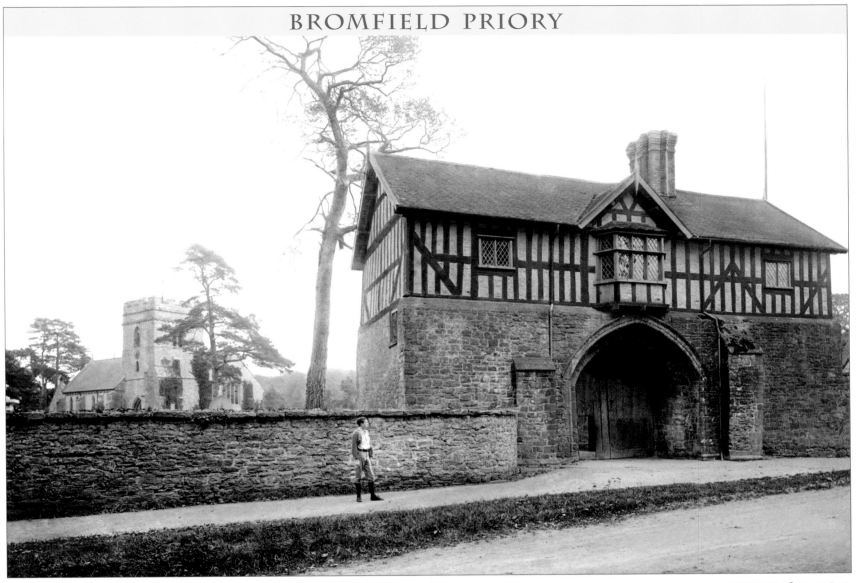

Above: BROMFIELD, THE PRIORY GATEHOUSE AND CHURCH 1892   30844P

St Mary's Church and its gatehouse are all that survive of a medieval Benedictine priory that was dissolved in the reign of Henry VIII. Before the Norman Conquest, Bromfield church was a rich minster served by twelve canons. By the early 12th century the canons were being gradually replaced by monks, and in 1155 Henry II issued a charter establishing a Benedictine priory, which seems to have been in fact attached to Gloucester Abbey; a Gloucester monk was installed as prior of Bromfield. Indeed, it appears that the canons were forced to become monks of Gloucester.

The priory took over the minster church, using the crossing (the later chancel) and the south transept; the lay congregation used the western end. The existing north-west tower was built in the early 13th century. In later years, morale declined; on one of his visits, the Bishop of Gloucester found that two of the monks 'were entirely given over to hunting and archery'! By the time of the Dissolution, it is possible that Bromfield Priory had become a small cell of just a few monks to run the estates. After the Dissolution, the priory was leased to Charles Foxe, who converted the conventual buildings into a private house – this was burnt down in the 17th century. Apart from the church, now the parish church, the only substantial part of the priory to survive is the gatehouse, a stone 14th-century structure with a timber-framed upper storey, possibly added after the Dissolution. It has been totally restored by the Landmark Trust.

SHREWSBURY ABBEY

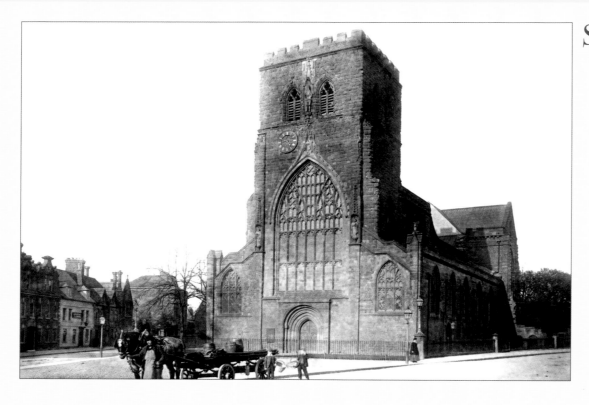

Shrewsbury Abbey was founded by Roger de Montgomery in 1083. He was one of William the Conqueror's generals, and built many castles, but the abbey is his best memorial. Inside there is an early tomb that is reputed to be his – he died three days after becoming a monk in the abbey he founded.

In medieval times Shrewsbury Abbey became extremely wealthy because it housed the shrine of the very popular St Winifred. The abbey was dissolved in the reign of Henry VIII, and much was then demolished. Fortunately the western end had always served as the local parish church, which is the only reason why the church was allowed to survive. In the 19th century it was restored and a new chancel was added. Pilgrims still come to Shrewsbury Abbey, but these days they are more likely to be seeking signs of Brother Cadfael, the fictional detective monk created by the writer Ellis Peters, whose exploits take place in 12th-century Shropshire.

Left: SHREWSBURY, THE ABBEY CHURCH 1891 28927P

HAUGHMOND ABBEY

This Augustinian abbey, dedicated to St John the Evangelist, is rare in that it was founded as a priory in the 1130s (there are traces of the original smaller church here) and then became an abbey in the 1150s. Most of the abbey church has disappeared, but much remains of the other buildings.

It stands near Shrewsbury on a steep hill, so that from it there are wonderful views towards the Welsh hills; the steepness of the slope meant that the normal abbey layout was impossible here, and the infirmary (or possibly the abbot's hall) and the abbot's lodging lie to the south, rather than on the east side of the cloister. Our photograph shows Haughmond's glory, the entrance to the chapter house: three deeply recessed Norman arches are linked by slim columns. The spaces between the columns were filled with carved figures in the 14th century, a most unusual feature.

Right: HAUGHMOND ABBEY, THE CHAPTER HOUSE 1891 28957

FINDING YOUR WAY AROUND AN ABBEY

All abbey plans are different in detail to a greater or lesser degree, yet all abbeys are laid out in a similar way, so that it is relatively simple to find one's way about. The heart of the abbey complex is the cloister, four covered walks around the square garth, or garden. Along the north side lies the abbey church, with two doors leading into it from each end of the north side. The ground floor of the east side is occupied by the chapter house, where the monks met every day to discuss the important matters in the life of the community. Here too may be found the sacristy, the vestry, a book cupboard or even a library, the parlour (where visitors could come to talk to a monk or the abbot), and a slype, or passage, leading to the infirmary behind the east side – the infirmary often had its own chapel, kitchen and latrines. Also on the east side is the day stair to the dorter (the monks' dormitory), which took up all the first floor; from the dorter a night stair leads down to the church, and at the other end is the reredorter, or latrines. On the south side may be found the warming house, the only room in the monastery with a fireplace; the novices' quarters; and the refectory, with a lavatorium, or wash basin, and cupboards for towels, outside in the cloister, with the kitchen beside the refectory. The western range was used as storerooms, and in Cistercian houses also as the living quarters for the lay brothers, manual workers who were not fully professed monks. The guesthouse would be near the main gatehouse.

PLAN OF A TYPICAL ABBEY (BASED ON FOUNTAINS)

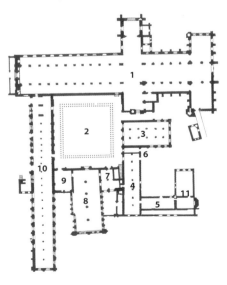

1. Abbey Church
2. Cloister
3. Chapter House
4. Dorter (first floor)
5. Reredorter
6. Slype leading to Infirmary
7. Warming House
8. Refectory
9. Kitchen
10. Storage / Lay brothers
11. Abbot's Residence

BUILDWAS ABBEY

Than this vale nothing can be more beautiful, or fuller of objects to gratify the eye and to afford subjects for a painter. Though having viewed Buildwas Abbey before, I could not abstain from making it another visit (a kind of duty to old, neglected people in their decline). There he stands, like all the rest, abandoned, neglected, filthy and a receptacle for carts, cows and pigs.

JOHN BYNG, 'RIDES ROUND BRITAIN' 1793
(EDITED BY D ADAMSON, FOLIO SOCIETY)

The abbey of St Mary and St Chad was a Cistercian abbey founded in 1135 by Roger de Clinton, Bishop of Coventry and Lichfield. The monastery was sited beside the Severn so that advantage could be taken of the trading links along the river. At one time the monks even ran their own ironworks. The abbey's buildings remained virtually unaltered throughout its life, so the present ruins are a good example of the Norman style. This photograph shows the remains of the nave, noted for its sturdy-looking round pillars that support a series of Norman arches.

Above: BUILDWAS ABBEY, FROM THE FERRY 1896   38115

SOUTHWELL MINSTER

The first impression is of too much light, the massive pillars and low arches giving a desire for deeper shadow and more gravity and mystery; but the huge west window lets in the broad daylight in a way the builders did not intend, and we must be content with the warm tint it gives to the yellow stone, and notice the soft shadows taken by the great round piers, the simple strength of the arches and of the aisle vaultings.

E GLAISTER, 1884

This superb minster church was founded before AD956; the present mainly Norman church was started in 1108 by the Archbishop of York, and the west towers were completed by about 1150. Pairs of Norman west towers rarely survive intact; this example is even rarer in having Norman leaded pyramidal roofs. Admittedly, these are replicas dating from 1880 – the originals burned down in 1711. This wonderful collegiate church (a cathedral since 1884) occupies the south-east corner of the town, and clergy houses line the north-east and south-west corners.

Southwell is truly a 'company town', with the townsfolk crammed into the north-west corner with their market place at the Burgage. Southwell has also expanded least around its historic core, and is the least-altered of the county's towns.

How fitting it is to view the cathedral from the bishop's garden (far left): the Gothic foliage carvings in the chapter house are justly famous. The Bishop's Manor, nestling in the lee of the minster, was built into the ruins of the 14th-century Bishop's Palace in 1907. It occupies the western half of the former palace, and the rest is open to the sky and used as a walled garden. The former palace was largely destroyed at the end of the Civil War after Charles I surrendered in Southwell in 1646.

Left: SOUTHWELL MINSTER, THE WEST GATE 1924   75665

Far left: SOUTHWELL MINSTER AND THE BISHOP'S MANOR 1920   69456

Glorious are its hillsides on a summer's day, its richly wooded landscape spreading out for many miles, and by the quiet road off Watling Street nature and man together have made a beauty unforgettable.

ARTHUR MEE,
'THE KING'S ENGLAND,
WARWICKSHIRE', 1949

Above left: MEREVALE ABBEY,
THE RECTORY WALLS 1924 76118
Below left: MEREVALE ABBEY,
DOORWAYS 1924 76119

MEREVALE ABBEY

Founded in 1148 by Robert de Ferrers, Earl of Derby, Merevale, a Cistercian abbey, was always a small house, with a population of about ten monks. The abbey was dissolved in 1538, and the building was quarried for farm buildings and a farmhouse. A working farm still occupies the site, although the medieval gate chapel is still in use as a church, and may contain features saved from the abbey. Hardly anything of the abbey itself now survives except what we see in these photographs. Here we see the outside wall of the refectory, rebuilt in the 13th century – note the unusual closely spaced buttresses. Inside the refectory, the pulpit stair is still almost complete.

The two 13th-century doorways in 76119 once led to the abbey kitchen and refectory. Beside the refectory door are the traces of the basin where the monks washed their hands before meals.

M R James cites Merevale's name (Mira Vallis) as an example of the pretty names which the Cistercians like to give their houses. He tells of Walter Map (in the 12th century), who hated the Cistercian order, and laughed at them for this custom. Other 'pretty' names included Casa Dei, Vallis Dei, and Portus Salutis.

LICHFIELD CATHEDRAL

Above: LICHFIELD CATHEDRAL 1969 L45064

A DIVINE JUDGEMENT?

In 1643, during the course of the Civil War, the Parliamentarians were keen to defeat the Royalists in the Midlands. Lord Brooke, one of Parliament's foremost commanders, advanced on Lichfield. Since the town had neither walls nor a castle, the Royalists had occupied the Cathedral Close; cannon surrounded the cathedral, and ammunition was stored within it. Lord Brooke besieged the garrison, and badly damaged the cathedral with a bombardment. On 4 March, Brooke prayed publicly that 'if the cause he were in were not right and just, he might be presently cut off'. He was shot dead through the eye later that day by a sniper posted on the central spire – the sniper was 'Dumb Dyott', a deaf and dumb local man. Lord Brooke had cursed cathedrals as 'the haunts of the Antichrist' on St Chad's day – St Chad was the patron saint of Lichfield – so the Royalists felt that his death was a divine judgement. However, the Royalist garrison surrendered three days later.

Above: LICHFIELD CATHEDRAL C1955 L45052   *Opposite above left:* LICHFIELD CATHEDRAL, THE WEST FRONT 1887 20222

Opposite below left: FRANCIS CHANTREY'S 'SLEEPING CHILDREN'   *Opposite below right:* LICHFIELD CATHEDRAL, THE CHOIR C1880 12833

Work on Lichfield Cathedral began in the late 12th century, and took about 150 years to complete, though additional work was undertaken during the 15th century. The three stone spires are known as the Ladies of the Vale. The cathedral was badly damaged during the Civil War: the central spire was all but destroyed, and much of the building was left roofless.

The west front (left) dates from the Decorated period, but most of this amazing display of sculpture is Victorian – only five statues high up on the north-west tower are original. The central doors have beautiful scrolled wrought iron hinges dating from c1300.

The 'Ladies of the Vale', as the spires of Lichfield have been poetically named, are exceptionally beautiful, whether seen from a neighbouring eminence rising above the roofs of the town, or from afar, in pleasant contrast with the woods and meadows of the neighbouring country.

Francis Chantrey's charming marble monument (below left) depicts the daughters of the Rev W Robinson, Prebendary of Lichfield, who died in 1812.

The bishop's throne and the choir stalls of Lichfield Cathedral (below right) were carved by George Evans, one of the novelist George Eliot's uncles (her real name was Mary Ann Evans). The high altar was restored in the 1850s by Sir George Gilbert Scott. One of the treasures of the cathedral is a volume of the Lichfield Gospels – there were originally two volumes, but one was lost during the Civil War. The surviving volume, dating from around AD730, is a manuscript copy, written in Latin in the Lindisfarne tradition, of the Gospels of Matthew, Mark and the early part of Luke. The manuscript is displayed in the chapter house from Easter to Christmas.

MALDON, BEELEIGH ABBEY

B eeleigh was a house of the Premonstratensians (White Canons). It was re-founded in 1180 (replacing an earlier house at Parndon); it became a private residence after the Dissolution. It was at this time that the timbered and brick-nogged wing on the left was put up. All that remains of the abbey today are the 11th-century south-east wing, which includes the chapter house, the dorter and its undercroft, and the parlour, all vaulted, and incorporated into the house. The main walls of the abbey were of 'pudding' stone, with Reigate stone used for the architectural details – this stone, though relatively easy to carve, did not weather well.

The site was rather dilapidated until a major restoration in 1912 by the architect Basil Ionides. Beeleigh's main claim to fame is that it belongs to the Foyle family; William Foyle founded the famous London bookshop, which was later run by his daughter Christina, and kept an important collection of books here. After Christina Foyle's death in 2002 the books, which included a first folio of the works of Shakespeare and a letter from Samuel Pepys, were sold for a record sum.

Left: MALDON, BEELEIGH ABBEY 1898 41522

Above: MALDON, BEELEIGH ABBEY, THE INTERIOR 1898 41523P

COLCHESTER, ST BOTOLPH'S PRIORY

Above: COLCHESTER, ST BOTOLPH'S PRIORY 1892   31528

St Botolph's was originally a Saxon religious community; but its historical importance lies in the fact that it was here that the first house of Augustinian canons in England was founded at the end of the 11th century. It lay outside the town walls, and never grew very large or important. The priory was dissolved under Henry VIII in 1535, but the church was taken over by the local parishioners. Many of the priory buildings disappeared through general decay and the quarrying of the stone, and the church was badly damaged during the bitter Civil War siege of Colchester in 1648.

What survives today is part of the west front and a large part of the nave. The drawing below shows the great west door, and above it the richly ornamented blind arcading of the facade; the building materials were Roman bricks and flint, reusing material from Colchester's extensive Roman remains. Originally the walls of the priory were plastered or rendered and lime-washed, then painted to mimic fine stonework blocks. Stone is not available locally, and the priory was presumably not wealthy enough to purchase any, so the builders made use of what they could find near to hand.

Sturdy circular piers extend down the nave, supporting typically Norman round-arched arcades (above left). Within the nave, centuries of burials had raised the ground level by about 4 feet. In 1912 the old tombs were removed, the ground level was lowered to Norman pavement level, and then the tombs were reinstated.

MEDIEVAL PLUMBERS

Among the workmen that haunted Grace Dieu (an Augustinian nunnery in Leicestershire) in these days (the early 1400s) was one called Richard Hyrenmonger. He came, we learn, from Donington, and the accounts prove that he must have had a good store of all kinds of nails, and keys, and bolts, judging by the variety he was able to produce. Under him worked John the Plumber, or rather two Johns the Plumber, senior and junior; and, like modern plumbers are wont

to do, they appear to have plagued Dame Petronilla and her assistant with their constant tinkering at the pipes and drains of the establishment. 'John the senior' and 'John the junior', for example, were six days mending 'le pype', for which they were paid 3s 4d; but apparently it was not properly done, for just after this, 'le pype' misbehaved itself again, and Dame Petronilla  *had to purchase a new brass pipe to bring the water to the door of the refectory, and the two Johns were at work again. Of course Richard the Ironmonger always found a lot of work for himself on the farm, so that what with one thing and another, Grace Dieu must have been a very comfortable inheritance for him.*

ABBOT GASQUET, 1904

ST OSYTH'S PRIORY

S t Osyth derives its name from the dedication of a local priory to a 7th-century princess, who built a nunnery here, of which she was the first abbess; she was beheaded by Danish invaders. St Osyth's Priory was founded in 1118 for Augustinian canons. They elected as their prior William de Corbeuil, who afterwards became Archbishop of Canterbury; at his death he left the priory large benefactions. In the 15th century the priory was largely rebuilt.

At the Dissolution the commissioners found among the plate and treasures 'the skull of Seynt Osithes closyed in sylver parcel gylte' as well as 'a croune of sylver gylte too sett apon the sayd skull garnysshyd with counterfett stones.'

The priory is now a private house. The photograph on the left shows the spectacular gatehouse, described by Kelly's Directory of 1933 as being 'of late Perpendicular date, elaborately covered with panelled work in flint and stone and consisting of an arched entrance with flanking towers: the whole is embattled and is supposed to have been erected about the reign of Henry VII' (1485–1509).

Kelly's Directory of 1933 continues: 'In the quadrangle is a range of old buildings in the Tudor style, with an octagonal observatory; there is also a lofty clock tower of modern date and two smaller ones; in the front of the mansion is a fine 16th century oriole window, in the wall of what was part of the abbot's lodgings, on which the initials of John Vyntoner, the last abbot but one, are frequently repeated, along with in every case a bunch of grapes, a tun of wine, and his initials J V and the date 1527'.

Left: ST OSYTH'S PRIORY 1895   35701

Above: ST OSYTH'S PRIORY 1895   35702

A MONK'S GAMES AND PASTIMES

The juniors and novices with their masters were permitted with leave to go out into the garden and other places to unbend in games and suchlike exercises proper to their age. In this way they were assisted when young to stand the severe strain of cloister discipline … The monk, it must be remembered, was in no sense 'a gloomy person'. There is hardly anything that would have interfered more with the purpose of his

life than any disposition to become a misanthrope. His calling was no bar to reasonable recreation. Thus at Durham we read of the greensward 'at the back of the house towards the water' where the younger members of the community played their games of bowls, with the novice-master as umpire. On the stone benches, too, in the cloisters at Canterbury, Westminster, Gloucester, and elsewhere, traces of the games played centuries ago by the young religious may still be seen in the holes and squares set out symmetrically, and oblongs divided by carefully-drawn cross-lines. Sometimes we read of hunting, contests of ball, and other games of chance. Archbishop Peckham was apparently somewhat shocked to find that the prior of Cokesford, in Norfolk, at times indulged in a game of chess with some of his canons. In other houses he found that dogs were kept and even stranger pets like apes, cranes, and falcons were retained in captivity by the religious.

ABBOT GASQUET, 1904

BURY ST EDMUNDS ABBEY

The building of the abbey church in Bury St Edmunds began in c1081 and took over 130 years to complete. The town was the resting place of the body of St Edmund (executed by the Danes in AD869 for refusing to give up his Christian faith), which had been brought to a monastery founded here by Siegbert, first Christian king of East Anglia in AD633. Bury became a major pilgrimage centre, which led King Canute to enlarge both the church and the town. William the Conqueror rebuilt the church on a lavish scale, and both the abbey and the town grew in wealth and status. The abbot controlled the town and viewed it as the abbey's 'gift shop'. The markets and fairs made Bury a leading commercial centre in medieval England. The tight hold of the abbot over the town led to disputes and conflict. In 1327, for example, the abbey was sacked by over 3,000 rioters, and the Norman abbey gate was destroyed. When the gate was rebuilt, it incorporated a guard room, a portcullis and arrow slits.

Left: BURY ST EDMUNDS ABBEY, THE RUINS 1898   41228

Top: BURY ST EDMUNDS ABBEY, THE GATEWAY 1898 41229
Above: BURY ST EDMUNDS, THE ABBOT'S BRIDGE

The abbey was closed by Henry VIII on 4 November 1539. The whereabouts of St Edmund's body is unknown, but it is most probable that the monks buried the remains somewhere within the abbey complex. All the abbey lands were sold. Houses had been built into the central arches of the west front of the abbey building by at least the 1660s. The Norman-style windows to the right of view 41228 (opposite) date from 1863, when this wing became the Probate Registry Office. In 1957 the Borough Council purchased the ruins from the Bristol family, as part of the scheme to turn the area into a cathedral close. The monuments were removed in 1958, and the area was laid to lawn. A statue of St Edmund by Dame Elizabeth Frink was placed here in 1976.

The original gate was probably a duplicate of the Norman tower; it was destroyed during the riot of 1327, and rebuilt in the Decorated style. The earlier gate stood to the left of its replacement (above), and the join in the wall shows its position. Within the niches on the front facade were statues, which were destroyed after the abbey was closed in 1539.

The 13th-century Abbot's Bridge (left) crosses the River Lark. Close by, the old abbey walls enclose the picturesque abbey gardens.

LEISTON ABBEY

North of Leiston are the flint and brick ruins of Leiston Abbey. The abbey of the White (Premonstratensian) Canons was transferred here from Minsmere in 1363; the canons brought all the Norman masonry from their original abbey and reused it on the new site. The abbey was rebuilt after a fire in 1382. The abbey is now home to Pro Corda, an organisation which runs chamber music courses for young people.

Of the abbey church, only the Lady Chapel remains as a complete building, a result of its usefulness for storing grain. It is fascinating to see, in this old photograph, how the abbey ruins are being used as farm buildings, a common fate of abbeys after the Dissolution. At Leiston, the south aisle of the church became a farmhouse.

Top: LEISTON, THE ABBEY 1894   33368

Right: LEISTON, THE ABBEY 1894   33370

Above: LEISTON, THE ABBEY 1922   72584

A DAY IN THE LIFE OF A MONK: MIDNIGHT TO 10AM

The great historian of the monasteries, Abbot Gasquet, says in his 'English Monastic Life' (1904): 'As the end and object of all forms of religious life was one and the same, the general tenor of that life was practically identical in all religious houses'. Thus most of the monastic orders followed a similar daily routine. At midnight, the monks were woken and descended the night stair to the church for Matins, the first service of the great cycle of prayer that St Benedict called 'Opus Dei', 'the work of God'. Matins was immediately followed by Lauds, 'the morning praises'; then at about 2am they went back to bed until about 6am, when they returned to the church for Prime. After a breakfast of bread and ale, the monks worked or read until 9am, the hour for the Chapter Mass, which was followed at 10am by Chapter, a daily meeting in the chapter house, where the business of the community was discussed.

DUNWICH PRIORY

Following ferocious storms between 1286 and 1288, the River Blyth's course changed, Dunwich's harbour was partly blocked, and huge areas of land were devoured by the sea, all of which marked the beginning of the decline of the town. The grey friars (Franciscans) had to move to this site for safety. Now the remains of the 13th-century priory are under threat once again from the sea.

The romantic ivy-covered ruins of the Franciscan priory are now the most substantial building left of the medieval town of Dunwich. The ravages of the North Sea have demolished the coastline, and legend says that on a quiet day the church bells of the drowned town can be heard ringing from under the sea. The priory ruins themselves will probably drop into the sea within the next 50 to 70 years.

I defy any one, at desolate, exquisite Dunwich, to be disappointed in anything. The minor key is struck here with a felicity that leaves no sigh to be breathed, no loss to be suffered … The biggest items are of course the two ruins, the great church and its tall tower, now quite on the verge of the cliff, and the crumbled, ivied wall of the immense cincture of the priory. These things have parted with almost every grace, but they still keep up the work that they have been engaged in for centuries and that cannot better be described than as the adding of mystery to mystery. This accumulation, at present prodigious, is, to the brooding mind, unconscious as the shrunken little Dunwich of today may be of it, the beginning and the end of the matter. I hasten to add that it is to the brooding mind only, and from it, that I speak. The mystery sounds for ever in the hard, straight tide, and hangs, through the long, still summer days and over the low, diked fields, in the soft, thick light.

HENRY JAMES, 1897

Far left: DUNWICH PRIORY, THE GATEWAY 1910   62050
Near left: DUNWICH PRIORY 1909   62049

NORWICH CATHEDRAL

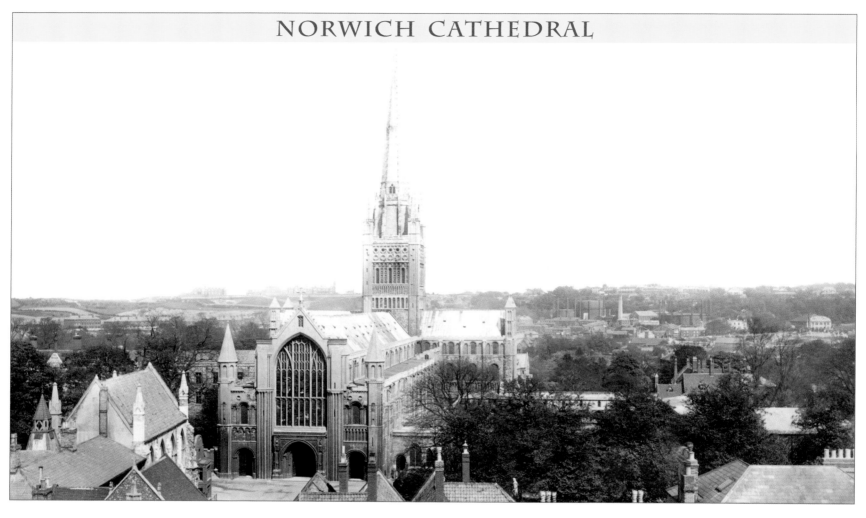

The city of Norwich has had its bishopric for 900 years; it was transferred from Thetford in 1094. The first Bishop of Norwich, Herbert de Losinga, had bought the Bishop of Thetford's mitre in 1091, along with the abbacy of Winchester, from William Rufus, who was quite happy to sell ecclesiastical appointments. Norwich had long been a thriving town. De Losinga arrived, and in the high-handed way of Norman aristocrats, promptly cleared a substantial part of the town to make his cathedral precinct.

The foundation stone for his great cathedral was laid in 1096, and the chancel was ready for dedication in September 1101. De Losinga died in 1119 and never saw his great project completed. The building was finally finished in 1145. The building is still essentially Norman, and only the great late 15th-century spire has materially changed distant views. It soars to 315 feet, the second highest spire in England after Salisbury. Its predecessor had been blown through the choir roof in a great gale in 1362; this also resulted in the building of the superb spacious clerestory of the choir.

There it spreads from north to south, with its venerable houses, its numerous gardens, its thrice twelve churches, its mighty mound, which, if tradition speaks true, was raised by human hands to serve as the grave-heap of an old heathen king, who sits deep within it, with his sword in his hand; and his gold and silver treasures about him. There is a grey old castle upon the top of that mighty mound; and yonder, rising three hundred feet above the soil, from among those noble forest trees, behold that old Norman master-work, that cloud-encircled cathedral spire, around which a garrulous army of rooks and choughs continually wheel their flight.

GEORGE BORROW (1803–1881)

The greatest and most successful and harmonious change to the Norman cathedral was the addition of stone vaults throughout, after a disastrous fire in 1463. The nave was done first, followed by the transepts and the choir, which were completed by 1500. It is astonishing that these intricate rib patterns and their glorious carved bosses complement the Norman work of 300 years before, but they undoubtedly do. The shafts and colonettes break the immense length of the nave and lead the eye up to the vaulted roof. This is one of the masterpieces of medieval English architecture.

Opposite above: NORWICH CATHEDRAL 1896 37349

Opposite below: DRAWING OF NORWICH CATHEDRAL AND PULLS FERRY

Left: NORWICH CATHEDRAL, THE NAVE LOOKING EAST 1891   28147

The Norman choir and nave aisles were vaulted in stone from the start (28153, left). The choir aisle vaults date from about 1100; they support the floor of the galleries above with their great arches.

The east walk of the cloisters was rebuilt first after a fire in 1272, and completed by 1314 (28154, opposite). The cloisters end at the extraordinarily ornate doorway into the nave, the Prior's Door, which dates from about 1310.

Many of Britain's cathedrals are set in a beautiful close, where the houses of the clergy cluster round. This scene is typical of so many closes (72598, above): charming houses, a harmonious mix of architectural styles and periods, stand in a quiet, peaceful lane near the cathedral.

Left: NORWICH CATHEDRAL, THE SOUTH CHOIR AISLE 1891   28153

Above: NORWICH CATHEDRAL PRECINCTS, HOOK'S WALK 1922   72598

Opposite: NORWICH CATHEDRAL, THE CLOISTERS, THE EAST WALK 1891   28154

During its eight centuries of existence on the spot where it still stands up so proudly, Norwich Cathedral has had some bad half-hours. In 1272 the citizens, infuriated by the exactions levied upon them by the prior, besieged the close and set the monastery on fire. The flames consumed a large portion of the archives of the monks and of the see, but the cathedral escaped. It was just ninety years after this that the great belfry was blown down, and almost exactly one hundred years after this latter calamity that another fire wrought much mischief. The last conflagration of which any record remains was in 1512, when the vestry was burnt, and all the vestments and 'ornaments' were consumed. The marks of this fire may still be seen in the triforium on the south of the presbytery, where the stone has been extensively discoloured by the fierce heat, and the course of the flames may easily be traced to this day by the ineffaceable marks they have left behind them. The central tower has twice been struck by lightning, once in 1271, and again in 1463.

AUGUSTUS JESSOPP, 1884

WYMONDHAM ABBEY

When they see this ruin from the road or the nearby railway, travellers are often puzzled by this church with towers at both ends. The west tower (left) was built by the parish in the mid 15th century; the central tower (right – the church originally extended to the right beyond the tower) was built by the priory in about 1400. These two towers symbolise the quarrels between the townsfolk and the monks (partly, apparently, about the bells) that went on for three centuries despite the Pope trying to make peace by allocating part of the church to the parish and part to the priory. Wymondham Priory was founded by William d'Abini, Earl of Arundel, in 1107. Never fully completed, the west tower is 142 feet 6 inches high; the north porch has a groined roof with well-carved bosses. The ruin to the south east of the church was the priory's chapter house.

The mainly Romanesque interior of the priory church is a contrast to the largely Perpendicular exterior. Dignified, sturdy Norman arches of the nave arcades and triforium support a spectacular hammerbeam roof complete with carved angels. The organ is 18th-century, and the gallery below it was erected in 1901.

Above: WYMONDHAM ABBEY 1891 29140

Visitors to Walsingham Priory came to see the Holy House, a miraculous recreation of the house where Jesus was brought up, together with other wonders. A devout noblewoman, Richeldis, had a vision of the Virgin Mary, who told her to copy her own home in Nazareth. A well on the site came to have healing properties, and Richeldis's son endowed 'England's Nazareth'. The shrine was founded in 1061, and destroyed in 1538. Every medieval king in England came here, and would have entered the priory grounds through this gate.

Above: WALSINGHAM PRIORY, THE GATEWAY 1922 72628

WALSINGHAM PRIORY

Above left: WALSINGHAM ABBEY, THE REFECTORY 1926 79300

Above right: WALSINGHAM, ST MARY'S CHURCH, THE SHRINE OF OUR LADY OF WALSINGHAM 1929 82039

Above: WALSINGHAM, THE PUMP AND OLD HOUSES 1929 82032P

Walsingham is built around the ruins of the Augustinian priory, celebrated for its shrine to Our Lady of Walsingham. Founded in 1149, the priory at Walsingham was renowned throughout Europe; it was an important place of pilgrimage, second only to Becket's tomb at Canterbury. All that is left today is a tantalising ruin in the grounds of Walsingham Abbey (the abbey is actually a mansion, which started life as the prior's house). The only remains of the priory church are the east window and piers of the west tower. Fragments of the refectory, the crypt or warming room and two old wells can also be seen. No traces remain of the original medieval holy shrine, although excavations in the 1960s revealed the location of the original Holy House to be just north of the nave - a small wooden plaque marks the site.

The town of Little Walsingham grew up to serve the many thousands of pilgrims that came to the priory, and pilgrims still come here in their thousands. The photograph on the left shows Common Place, a square in the High Street; the 16th-century octagonal pump house has a brazier on its roof, 'The Beacon', which used to be the only street lighting in Walsingham. The pinnacle that used to top the pump house was broken off in the 1900s.

In 1922 the parish priest of the church of St Mary the Virgin at Walsingham, Fr Hope Patten, discovered a medieval seal of the old priory in the British Museum. At its centre was an image of Our Lady, which is presumed to be a representation of the image at the priory that was destroyed at the Reformation. Fr Patten had a new wooden statue made to place in the church, and pilgrims began to return to Walsingham, in such numbers that a new shrine church was built in 1931. Since then the shrine has once more become a place of peace to many pilgrims worshipping there.

WEST RUNTON, BEESTON PRIORY

Above: WEST RUNTON, BEESTON PRIORY 1894 33319

This ancient priory of Augustinian canons was founded around 1216 by Margaret Cressy. Apart from benefactions, the canons also received a share of the profits made from shipwrecks, and any other items of value which were washed ashore between Runton and Beeston. The religious life in the Middle Ages was not always one of ordered calm: in 1317 Canon John de Walsam of Beeston attacked and wounded his bishop with a sword, and was sent in disgrace to Rome for his case to be settled by Pope John XXII. Later that year, when the bishop had recovered from his wounds, the Pope granted de Walsam absolution. Another flouter of authority was Canon Thomas Taverner: when Bishop Goldwell visited Beeston in 1494, he discovered that Taverner was absent without leave, and again when Bishop Nicke visited in 1514, Taverner was away in Norwich without permission. At the Dissolution, there were only three canons at Beeston. It is said that a tunnel runs from the Dunstable Arms Inn at Beeston to the priory.

 A DAY IN THE LIFE OF A MONK: 11AM TO 7PM

The office of Terce was followed by High Mass, celebrated with some ceremony at 11am, and then came dinner at 12 noon: soup, bread, and vegetables, often with cheese, eggs and fruit, washed down with ale – meat and fish were only eaten on feast days. During the meal one monk would read from the scriptures or the writings of holy men. After dinner the monks had some free time, when they could rest or read; then at 2pm came the next service, Nones, then more work. The service of Vespers was at 4pm, again followed by work. A light supper was served at 6pm, consisting of one course followed by a pittance (fruit, nuts and the like), and next came the evening reading, the Collation, in the chapter house, and then evening prayer, Compline, at 7pm. After Compline, the monks went to bed. (This was the approximate routine in summer; the winter timetable was slightly different.)

CASTLE ACRE

William de Warenne was William the Conqueror's son-in-law; he built the castle which gave the village of Castle Acre its name. He founded this Cluniac priory in 1089 – his father had founded the first Cluniac monastery in England at Lewes. Here we see the glorious west front of the church, a prime example of Norman decorative detailing. The large west door is flanked by two smaller doors, and rich interlaced blind arcades of varied heights cover the walls. The blind windows on either side of the great west window (a later alteration from the Perpendicular period) have fish-scale patterns. The priory stands in fields by the River Nar, prominent thanks to the white stone and flint in which it is built. The domestic buildings are quite well preserved, particularly the reredorter, or latrine block, which stands over a running stream – fresh water and safe sewage disposal were a vital part of monastic planning.

Left: CASTLE ACRE PRIORY, THE WEST FRONT 1891 29113

Above: CASTLE ACRE, THE OLD GATE 1891 29111

ELY CATHEDRAL

Ely Cathedral, which can be seen from up to twenty miles away on a clear day, is one of the most stirring sights in Fenland. Etheldreda founded a religious community for women here in AD673: she died just six years later. Like so many of the Fenland monasteries, it was destroyed by marauding Danes in AD870. It was re-founded as a male religious house following the rule of St Benedict. Tradition says that some of the monks were unwilling to embrace the newly imposed rule of celibacy; they were punished by being turned into eels! Etheldreda herself gave a new word to the language. She was known as Audrey, and the cheapness of stuff sold at the annual fair at Ely, known as St Audrey's Fair, gave rise to the word 'tawdry'.

Ely Cathedral is the fourth longest cathedral in England (535 feet) and has a unique eight-sided central tower. The earliest major piece of vaulting in the cathedral is in the Galilee Porch, dating from about 1250. The cathedral's choir stalls are 14th-century, and all have misericords, wooden brackets on which the monks could lean during long services. They include wonderfully imaginative carvings, such as monkeys, a bear, a man falling off a horse and a woman beating a fox.

We enter and stand on the threshold. Under favourable conditions of light and shade, we doubt if a more striking architectural view than this can be presented to the eye. The vista is unbroken as far as the eastern wall, 517 feet from us, save by light screen-work of open design. Three tall lancets, surmounted by five others, ingeniously worked into the curves of the stone vaulting, terminate and close in the distant point in which the long lines of walls, roof, and floor are brought together, with an effect surpassing in solemn grandeur, as we think, any composition in which one vast window, as at York or Carlisle, is the chief feature. Tall and narrow arches carry the eye upwards, and give an impression of loftiness which will bear comparison even with that conveyed by Cologne or Amiens, and to which the narrowness of the central alley contributes.

W E DICKSON, 1884

After passing through the Galilee Porch, the visitor is greeted with this stunning view (above): three storeys of Norman arches lead the eye to the central space and the choir beyond.

The photograph above gives a close view of the wooden octagonal turret rising out of the larger stone octagonal tower. The octagon was built to the design of the cathedral sacrist Adam de Walsingham; it replaced the central tower of the cathedral, which fell down in 1322.

Above: ELY CATHEDRAL, THE NAVE, LOOKING EAST 1891 28191
Left: ELY, THE VIEW FROM THE WEST TOWER OF THE CATHEDRAL C1955 E34071
Opposite: ELY CATHEDRAL FROM THE MEADOWS 1898 40867

The wonderful doorway below (28190) dates from about 1140. Above the door is a carving of Christ in majesty, with an angel on each side. The carvings on the door surrounds include depictions of various people at work and the signs of the zodiac. Like the woodcarvers of the choir stalls, the stonemasons were clearly encouraged to use their imaginations!

Below: ELY CATHEDRAL, THE PRIOR'S DOOR 1891 28190 (DETAIL)

Peterborough is too perfect for my pencil.

JOHN SELL COTMAN, 1804

PETERBOROUGH CATHEDRAL

This view shows the west front of the cathedral, which rose from the monastery originally founded in the 7th century by Peada, the Anglo-Saxon King of Mercia. Saxulf became the first abbot in AD675. The core of the present cathedral was the abbey church begun by the Benedictine Abbot Martin in 1118. A visit to its altar was considered equivalent to a visit to Rome. The abbey church was built between 1118 and 1258 in the local Barnack oolitic limestone; the nave, eleven bays long, had large piers. The building characterises the best of Norman workmanship and is little altered since Norman times; the only additions are the Early English porch and spires and the Perpendicular retro-choir, the 'New Building', with its exuberant fan vaulting, stylistically similar to the fan vaulting at King's College, Cambridge. The present building is one of only three churches in Europe with an early painted wooden ceiling in its nave; of those three, Peterborough's is by far the biggest. Mary, Queen of Scots was buried in Peterborough Cathedral (her body was later moved to Westminster Abbey), and so was Henry VIII's first queen, Katherine of Aragon. Her tomb was destroyed in 1643. In 1895 a slab of Irish marble to commemorate her was provided and paid for by all the women in Peterborough named Katherine in honour of the unhappy queen.

Below we see the arches of the monastery infirmary, the forerunner of medical care in Peterborough.

Left: PETERBOROUGH CATHEDRAL AND THE MARKET SQUARE 1904 51544P

Above: PETERBOROUGH, THE INFIRMARY ARCHES 1890 24444

After dinner we took a walk. Peterborough is a very small town gathered in front of its glorious minster. It is the cathedral, and nothing else. We soon came to the market place, on one side of which is the guildhall, now used for a butter shop, beneath the lower pillars. Opposite to it is a stone gateway, which is the entrance to the close. As we entered the close, the world seemed shut out, as it always does inside these monastic retreats. Eternal peace is within their gates, and upon me the effect of the three vast arches of the western facade was more sublime and magnificent than that of any architecture I have yet seen in England. I was wholly unprepared for the vastness and splendor of this church. No one had ever spoken of it to me, and I had never read about it. I believe there is no other facade like this in the country – the arches being much higher than that we so wondered at in Furness Abbey – three arches, perfectly uninjured. I did not know before what a grand power lay in a lofty curve, and words can never convey an idea of it. The first impression was that those arches had more to do with Heaven than earth. Though the line returns again to the same level from which it rises, yet it seems to have been transfigured as it soared and sang in its circuit. They are the emblem of a saint's soul, whose visible form still exists. He stands on the earth, but his spirit has ascended into another world, and remains there, in truth, though he is yet with us in mortal guise. They are an image of endless aspiration in constant rest.

SOPHIA HAWTHORNE, 1857

Left:
PETERBOROUGH
CATHEDRAL,
THE SLYPE 1919
69085

Right:
PETERBOROUGH
CATHEDRAL,
THE HIGH ALTAR
1894   34827

A slype (69085, above) is a medieval word for a covered passage, often leading from an abbey church to its monastic buildings or from the cloister to the buildings beyond, such as the infirmary.

In the photograph above we see the original apsidal end of the cathedral with its Norman arches. Beyond is the Perpendicular retro-choir. The bishop's throne, the choir stalls, the marble floor, and the high altar were all designed by J L Pearson, the distinguished Victorian architect.

CROWLAND, CROYLAND ABBEY

CROWLAND,
CROYLAND ABBEY 1894
34831

Nothing can be more noble, more Gothic or more elegantly carved than the front (now tottering) of Crowland Abbey, a beauty of the richest workmanship. My eyes gloried in beholding, whilst my heart sickened at the destruction ... So much for Crowland. I am glad to have seen thee in thy last decline; it is like the comfort of having taken leave of a friend upon his deathbed.

JOHN BYNG, 'RIDES ROUND BRITAIN', 1790
(EDITED BY D ADAMSON, FOLIO SOCIETY)

Croyland Abbey, in the Middle Ages the richest in Lincolnshire, is now a remarkable fragment; the north aisle of the abbey church is now the parish church with a monumental 15th-century tower capped by a squat spire, and all the monastic buildings have vanished. The remains of the rest of the abbey church are a tantalising glimpse of an opulent past. St Guthlac came to this island in the fens in the 7th century, seeking a holy and ascetic life; he dressed in skins, and the only nourishment he took was a scrap of barley bread and a little muddy water once a day. Pilgrims came to him for counsel, including Ethelbald, pretender to the throne of Mercia, who in Guthlac's honour laid the foundation stone of the abbey in AD716. A Danish raid and a fire meant that the abbey had to be rebuilt twice; the west front was altered in the 13th century and again in the 15th, when the nave with its aisles was reconstructed.

LINCOLN CATHEDRAL

Left:
LINCOLN
CATHEDRAL
AND STONEBOW
1890   25654P

Opposite left:
LINCOLN
CATHEDRAL,
THE CHOIR
LOOKING WEST
1890   25641

Opposite right:
LINCOLN
CATHEDRAL,
THE WEST DOOR
C1879   12448

THE WORK OF A MONK

The work of a monk consisted of arduous hours of prayer, and also of 'lectio divina', holy reading - the study of the scriptures, the lives of the saints, and the writings of holy men and philosophers. Writers and painters created manuscripts, and the juniors and novices practised public reading and singing. It must be remembered, however, that a monastery was often not just a religious community, but the equivalent of a modern commercial company. Most monasteries owned land – some owned thousands of acres – which they farmed efficiently. Their outlying farms were called granges, from the French for granary. The Cistercians in particular were famed for their farming skills, especially sheep farming, and exported their wool as far afield as Italy. Within the monastery precinct would be gardens, fishponds, a mill, a brewhouse, and stables, which all had to be managed. The monks might well run other enterprises – at Blanchland, for instance, the Premonstratensian canons ran a silver refinery and a fulling mill, at Rievaulx the Cistercians had a fulling mill too, and also a tannery, and the monks of Durham produced timber from their woodlands and coal from their mines.

Beautiful beyond all English cathedrals and minsters, with the exception, perhaps, of St Cuthbert's mighty fane at Durham. There is a brilliant passage in one of Mr. Froude's 'Short Studies' which must have been penned with Lincoln vividly present to his mind's eye. Nowhere do you feel more powerfully as you approach that 'the cathedral, with its huge towers, majestically beautiful, is the city'. Nowhere is the contrast more striking between the vastness of the edifice, standing out clear and sharp with its exquisite beauty of outline and refined harmony of proportions, and 'the puny dwelling-places of the citizens', which 'creep at its feet' and stream down the hillside in motley confusion. Nowhere do you more vividly realise that 'the cathedral is the one object which possesses the imagination and refuses to be eclipsed'.   EDMUND VENABLES, 1884

The seat of the Anglo-Saxon see of Dorchester on Thames was moved by William the Conqueror to Lincoln. Remigius, who had been bishop since 1067, claimed control of Lindsey as well as the rest of the huge bishopric that ran from the Thames to the Humber, a claim hotly disputed by the Archbishops of York. However, Remigius moved north in 1072 and immediately started work on his new cathedral. It had a giant 'westwork' which survives as the lower part of the present west end. Its original design and purpose is still controversial: historians currently suggest that it may have been a fortified rectangular bishop's palace. Its three giant arched niches flanked by smaller ones survive, and it is certainly a most puzzling structure.

Finished by 1092, the minster church east of the west block has been replaced. Remigius's west end was, however, retained and altered and surmounted by towers raised by the mighty Bishop Alexander after a fire in 1141. The rest of Alexander's work was swept away by the great Gothic church that followed. This rebuild was necessitated by a spectacular earthquake in 1185: from this tragedy one of Europe's most impressive cathedrals emerged, initially under St Hugh of Avalon, bishop from 1186 to 1200. His eastern transept and choir survive, but his east apse was replaced by the sublime Angel Choir, mainly to house his relics and to accommodate the flow of pilgrims following his canonisation. The nave had been rebuilt by the 1230s, and the longer cathedral of St Hugh burst through the Roman east city wall. This bald description of events does little justice to the wonderful, awe-inspiring qualities of the cathedral, surmounted by its three richly crocketed towers. These were once crowned by lead-clad timber spires, which raised the central tower's height to an astonishing 530 feet, the highest in Europe. This blew down in 1548, but the western spires survived until 1807. The magnificent west front still retains the rough ashlar stones of the earliest cathedral structure; its three round-arched doorways can still be seen framed clearly within the later more elaborate façade (above right).

THE LINCOLN IMP

The builders of the shrine of St Hugh wanted pilgrims to have in mind the ever-present danger of evil, so they included a reminder of the devil within the Angel Choir. A carving (L49078, below), in the form of a small diabolical creature, was placed high above the left shoulder of pilgrims as they knelt to pray. The creature has become world-famous as the Lincoln Imp. There are many fanciful stories about the imp; perhaps the most popular is that the imp was having so much fun causing trouble in the cathedral that the angels turned him to stone, although other stories seem to emphasise that he was blown into the cathedral during a tremendous storm. Whatever the myths, the imp has become a symbol of Lincoln.

Above: LINCOLN CATHEDRAL,
THE LINCOLN IMP C1955 L49078

CHESTER CATHEDRAL

Top: CHESTER CATHEDRAL, THE WEST FRONT 1888 20577P

Above: CHESTER CATHEDRAL, THE CHOIR LOOKING WEST 1888 20583

[There] is a certain irresistible regret that so much of its hoary substance should give place to the fine, fresh-coloured masonry with which Mr Gilbert Scott, ruthless renovator, is so intelligently investing it. The red sandstone of the primitive structure, darkened and devoured by time, survives at many points in frowning mockery of the imputed need of tinkering. The great tower, however – completely restored – rises high enough to seem to belong, as cathedral towers should, to the far-off air that vibrates with the chimes and the swallows, and to square serenely, east and west and south and north, its embossed and fluted sides.

HENRY JAMES, 1872

Built of red sandstone, Chester Cathedral was founded in 1092 as a Benedictine abbey on the site of an earlier Saxon church dedicated to St Werburgh. St Werburgh was a late 7th-century Saxon princess and a daughter of King Wulfhere of Mercia. Werburgh was later appointed supervisor of all the nunneries in Mercia, and died at Trentham in AD699. In AD874 St Werburgh's remains were transferred to Chester to prevent them from falling into the hands of Danish invaders. Parts of the Norman church can still be seen, though much of the present cathedral dates from the 13th to the 16th centuries. At the Dissolution the building was saved from destruction when it was chosen as the cathedral for the newly formed diocese of Chester. In the 19th century, a careful restoration programme was undertaken by Sir George Gilbert Scott, who added battlements, pinnacles and buttresses, but he yearned most of all to top the tower with a tall spire.

Intricately carved choir stalls from 1380 provide a rich and enclosed setting for the choir (opposite below right). The ironwork suspended cross seen in this photograph – it was designed by Sir George Gilbert Scott – was removed in the early years of the 20th century, possibly because it was considered to be too 'high church'; it is now in the parish church of Dunham-on-the-Hill.

The Dean's seat (below right) is just one of the many superb examples of wood carving in the choir stalls, where bench ends, misericords and canopies are intricately and beautifully carved. There are only two other places where the quality of the wood carving is comparable to Chester: one is Lincoln Cathedral, and the other is Beverley Minster.

Herman Melville described Chester's misericords in 1856: '*These projections on the seat are each and all of them carved with curious devices, no two alike. The guide showed us one, representing, apparently, the first quarrel of a new-married couple, wrought with wonderful expression. Indeed, the artist never failed to bring out his idea in the most striking manner; as for instance, Satan under the guise of a lion, devouring a sinner bodily, and again in the figure of a dragon, with a man half-way down his gullet, the legs hanging out. The carver may not have seen anything grotesque in this, nor have intended it at all by way of joke; but certainly there would appear to be a sort of grim mirthfulness in some of the designs. One does not see why such fantasies should be strewn about the holy interior of a cathedral, unless it were intended to contain everything that belongs to the heart of man, both upward and downward.*'

Top: CHESTER CATHEDRAL, A MISERICORD 1913   66103 (DETAIL)

Above: CHESTER CATHEDRAL, THE DEAN'S SEAT 1913 66108A

CHESTER, ST JOHN'S PRIORY

Above: CHESTER, ST JOHN'S PRIORY 1913   66100
Above right: CHESTER, ST JOHN'S PRIORY 1888   20625
Below right: CHESTER, ST JOHN'S CHURCH INTERIOR 1888   20621

Construction of St John's Priory was begun about 1075–76 when the Bishop of Lichfield, Peter de Leia, transferred the seat of his diocese to Chester. There was an earlier Saxon church on the site; according to local legend, King Harold survived the battle of Hastings, lived out the remainder of his life in seclusion at Chester, and was buried in St John's. The choir and chancel were destroyed in 1470 when the central tower collapsed. The north-west tower, rebuilt around 1523, collapsed in 1573 and destroyed the west front. Following the collapse of the north-west tower, a detached belfry was erected on its site, but this too collapsed in 1881 and wrecked the north porch. The north porch was restored in the Early English style in 1882. The ruins of the choir and chancel still stand picturesquely next to the church. It is possible to wander around the romantic ivy-covered ruins, where an ancient oak coffin is set into the stones high up on one wall; inscribed on it are the appropriate words 'Dust to Dust'.

The present church of St John occupies the nave of the former priory. The exterior, very much restored in the 1860s, belies the glorious interior, which we see here – photograph 20621 (above right) shows the crossing, which amazingly outlasted the two collapsed central towers. This is all Norman and Early English work, sturdy, light and uncluttered. The mighty round piers of about 1095 have scalloped capitals and double-stepped arches, above them is the triforium of about 1195. The styles of three centuries work harmoniously together.

Whalley Abbey was founded in 1172 in Stanlaw, Cheshire; the land around was susceptible to flooding, so the monks moved here to land given by the lord of the manor of Clitheroe in 1296. The abbey took nearly 200 years to complete – building materials were scarce. However, throughout the 14th and 15th centuries there were between 20 and 30 monks here, and by Tudor times the abbey was quite prosperous. In 1536, John Paslew, the last abbot, was involved in the Pilgrimage of Grace (a protest movement against the religious changes instigated by Henry VIII), and he and two monks were executed in 1537. At the Dissolution, Whalley was seized by the Crown. Now the most impressive remains are the two gateways; the ruins of the chapter house remain, and some of its original tiles have been found.

The abbot's kitchen had three fireplaces (far left). Ahead is part of the mansion which was converted from the abbot's house and the abbey infirmary.

Medieval monks were always careful to construct efficient and hygenic water and drainage systems in their monasteries. Here we see the drain under the monks' latrine, which was next to their dormitory (left). This drain was always sited downstream from the water supply for the kitchen and the wash basin in the cloister.

Top: WHALLEY ABBEY, PART OF THE PRECINCT WALL 1894   34336
Above: WHALLEY ABBEY, THE ABBOT'S KITCHEN 1894   34335
Right: WHALLEY ABBEY, ARCHES OVER THE DRAIN 1895   35710

WHALLEY ABBEY

MALTBY, ROCHE ABBEY 1893   31978P

ROCHE ABBEY

Founded in 1147, Roche Abbey was a colony of Newminster in Northumberland, itself a daughter of the great Cistercian abbey of Fountains. The abbey took its name from a cross-like rock that was already an object of pilgrimage for the faithful. In 1538 Roche Abbey was surrendered to the Crown and destroyed. David Knowles in 'Bare Ruined Choirs' (1976) recounts stories of monks 'seeking to raise cash on the contents of their cells, and the natives filching missals to patch the covers of their waggons, and pulling iron hooks out of the walls. One of those favourable to the old religion and a friend of the monks, who had bought much of the timber of the church, when asked long after how he could bring himself to do it, expressed the view of his contemporaries when he replied: "I did see all would away; and therefore I did as others did".'

The choir stalls were fired to melt lead, and timber and stone were sold off – the great building was reduced to little more than a quarry. Michael Sherbrook, rector of Wickersley, wrote: 'All things of price either spoiled carted away or defaced to the uttermost … nothing was spared but the oxhouses and swinecoates and other such houses of office, that stood without the walls.' The main ruins comprise parts of the east walls of the transepts, part of the chancel and a vaulted gatehouse.

MONASTERY OFFICIALS 1

The abbot had absolute power; the title means father, and St Benedict says that 'an abbot who is worthy to have charge of a monastery ought always to remember by what title he is called', and that 'in the monastery he is considered to represent the person of Christ'. His second-in-command was the prior, whose concern was discipline within the monastery, and he had one or more sub-priors to assist him. The cantor or precentor was in charge of church music and ceremonies; he had to arrange all the complex church rituals, and with the help of his assistant, the succentor, he had to rehearse the singers. The precentor was also chief librarian and archivist, and had to supply the writers with their ink and parchment. The sacrist's responsibility was the sacred vessels, the vestments, and the fabric of the church; he was also in charge of candle making and lamps, and he had to keep the monks' cemetery in good order. The cellarer took care of food, drink and fuel supplies, and was in charge of all the servants and the outlying granges, or farms.

THE OFFERING OF A CHILD TO AN ABBOT (13TH CENTURY)

RIPON CATHEDRAL

Stonemasons and glaziers from France and Italy built St Wilfrid's Church on this site in AD672, one of the first stone churches in England. This church was destroyed by the English king in AD948, but its tiny crypt still exists beneath the present cathedral, a rare survival of Saxon ecclesiastical building. The crypt may have been used to store religious relics which St Wilfrid brought back from Rome. A second church was built, but this too was destroyed, this time by the Normans. Thomas of Bayeux, the first Norman Archbishop of York, built a third church, which was followed by the grand building we see today from 1180. The stunning Early English west front was added in 1220. Some alteration and rebuilding took place in the late 15th century, and the misericords (see 67323) were carved at this time. The minster finally became a cathedral in 1836.

Ripon Cathedral has associations with Wilfred Owen, one of the finest poets of the First World War. After a period of convalescence after suffering from shell shock, he was posted in 1918 to Ripon, where he wrote 'Futility' and 'Strange Meeting', among other poems. He spent his 25th birthday in the cathedral. Later that year he returned to France, where he was killed in the last week of the war.

 DOWN THE RABBIT HOLE INTO WONDERLAND

RIPON, THE GRIFFIN AND RABBITS MISERICORD 1914 67323

 Lewis Carroll (1832–98) – his real name was Charles Lutwidge Dodgson – was the son of one of the first canons of the cathedral, and visited his father here in Ripon over a span of 20 years. He was inspired by cathedral carvings of a lion, an elephant on the back of a turtle, and the curious creatures carved on the misericords in the choir; in 67323, we see a griffin chasing two rabbits – one of them is disappearing down a rabbit hole. He first conceived his story of Alice in Wonderland in July 1862, after ten years of visits to Ripon and its magnificent cathedral.

It is a very picturesque object, whether viewed from the country above the river Ure, which adds so much to the beauty of the neighbourhood, or whether approached from Kirkgate, with its fine west front before us.

H D CUST-NUNN, 1884

Opposite: RIPON CATHEDRAL AND THE WEIR C1885 18316

Above left: RIPON CATHEDRAL, FROM THE NORTH-WEST C1885 18319

Below left: RIPON CATHEDRAL, THE LIBRARY C1885 18338

YORK MINSTER

York is a pleasant and beautiful city. The cathedral is a gothic building. The only deficiency I find at York minster, is the lowness of the great tower, or its want of a fine spire upon it, which, doubtless, was designed by the builders.

DANIEL DEFOE,
'A TOUR THROUGH THE WHOLE ISLAND OF GREAT BRITAIN', 1724

Begun during the reign of King John and finally completed in 1472, York Minster stands on a site previously occupied by the praetorium of a Roman fort and by Saxon churches; the earliest of these was a small wattle oratory constructed for the baptism of Edwin, King of Northumbria, in AD627. The minster is one of the largest cathedrals of England, and the western towers are 196 feet high. Between 1829 and 1984 there were three fires at the minster; the first was caused deliberately, the second by a careless workman, and the third by lightning. All three caused damage and loss, and much restoration has had to be carried out.

St William's College (on the right of 65443, below), a beautiful jettied building, was first built for the minster's chantry priests in about 1465, and stands just under the glorious east end of the minster. The college was much altered in the 16th and 17th centuries, when it was divided up; when Charles I moved his court to York during the Civil War, the royal printing press was housed here. By the 19th century it had fallen on hard times and had become ramshackle slum tenements. A benefactor, Francis Green, saved it and then sold it to the council, who restored it. St William's College is said to be haunted by the ghost of a 17th-century murderer.

Left: YORK MINSTER, FROM THE SOUTH-WEST 1909 61705
Above: YORK MINSTER, THE EAST END AND ST WILLIAM'S COLLEGE 1913 65443

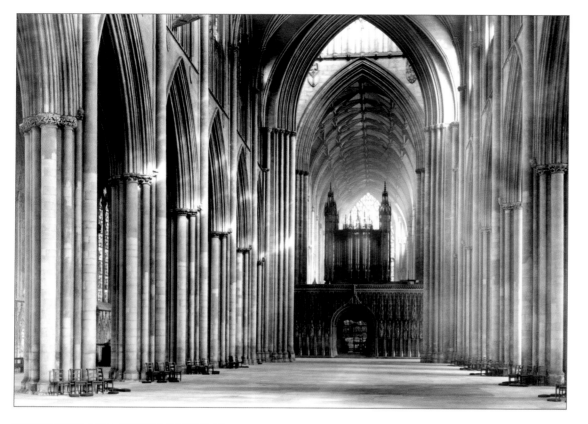

It has the largest nave in any English cathedral, and, as in the case of that other, St Peter's, in a sunnier city, the proportions are so exquisite that the eye takes some time to realise the size. All is so simple, so grand, and fault-finders add 'so cold'. Perhaps there is a little want of colour, but where form is so perfect one could scarcely wish, even for the sake of warmth, to risk the loss of purity.

CONSTANCE ALDERSON, 1884

The soaring nave (top left), the widest in England, was begun in the 1280s; by the 1330s the outer roof was built, but the technical difficulties of constructing a vaulted roof of stone over such a wide space meant that wood had to be used instead. The work took a long time to complete – oak timber was scarce, and the master carpenter lost his head for heights; it was not until the 1360s that the vaulting was finished. In this photograph, we can just see a dragon's head projecting from the nave wall (left of centre at the extreme top of the picture. It is also shown in the photo to the left). It has a hole in its neck through which a chain could pass, so perhaps it was a mechanism for raising the font cover. Beyond the ornate 15th-century screen is the Perpendicular choir, lit by the great east window of 1405, the largest expanse of medieval glass ever to survive.

The monument to Sir William Gee (61713, below left), secretary to King James I and a member of his privy council, was erected by his widow, Mary, after his death in 1611. It shows Sir William, his two wives and six children at prayer.

Top left: YORK MINSTER, THE NAVE 1907 58668

Far left: YORK MINSTER, THE GEE MONUMENT 1909 61713 (DETAIL)

Above left: YORK MINSTER, THE NAVE, THE DRAGON 1925 78954

Below left: YORK MINSTER, THE CROZIER 1908 59792

JERVAULX ABBEY

Part of some chapels remain, and much for the observation of an antiquary. But all the doorways being stoned up, I had to climb over walls and force my way through nettles and brambles. What has ruined this place, with most others, has been the building a house near the ruins. This mansion has now dwindled into a farmhouse, before which is a gateway of approach, an attempt at the Gothic, but of no very ancient date. The great old barns are now falling down. The view from the terrace, above the farmhouse, is very beautiful, affording a long meander of the River Ure.

JOHN BYNG
'RIDES ROUND BRITAIN', 1792 (EDITED BY D ADAMSON,
FOLIO SOCIETY)

Jervaulx lies peacefully on the banks of the River Ure (the name is a Frenchification of Yorevale, valley of the Ure). Land for the abbey was given to the monks by Conan, son of Alan the Red, who built Richmond Castle. The abbey was established in 1156, and it gained its revenue from sheep breeding and mining for coal and iron. The monks were the first to produce Wensleydale cheese, using sheep's milk. Jervaulx was destroyed in 1537 by Henry VIII – the last abbot was hanged at Tyburn for his part in the Pilgrimage of Grace – see box on page 126. King Henry took his revenge on Jervaulx by blowing up the abbey church with gunpowder.

At Jervaulx, the decision has been taken not to tidy the ruins up too much and to allow wild flowers and climbing plants to scramble over the old stones. The result is beautiful and charming, and a refreshing change from the sometimes stark ruins of other abbeys; today, the ruins look not very different from the way they looked in the 1890s. Photograph 33125 shows what is left of the chapter house, with its six steps down from the cloisters, large round-arched windows, and pillars that once supported the vaulted roof.

Top right: JERVAULX ABBEY 1893 33125
Above left: JERVAULX ABBEY, STONE DETAIL 2004 J3701K
Above right: JERVAULX ABBEY, DOORWAY 2004 J3702K

Abbey! for ever smiling pensively,
How like a thing of nature dost thou rise
Amid her loveliest works! as if the skies,
Clouded with grief, were arched thy roof to be,
And the tall trees were copied all from thee!

EBENEZER ELLIOTT, C1850

Near right: FOUNTAINS ABBEY 1886 18352

Above: FOUNTAINS ABBEY, STUDLEY ROYAL, THE WATER GARDEN C1874
7391

Far right: FOUNTAINS ABBEY, THE UNDERCROFT TO THE WEST RANGE
C1873 6650

FOUNTAINS ABBEY

In 1132 a small group of monks from St Mary's Abbey, York, disenchanted by their abbey's laxity, and inspired by the strict Cistercian rule, settled here in the remote valley of the River Skell. Fountains Abbey eventually became very wealthy thanks to the wool trade; the monks owned vast estates where they reared sheep. At one time, Fountains had over 600,000 acres of land given over to wool production. The wealth of the abbey enabled the monks to spend money on ever more grand and extensive buildings.

The ruins date from the 12th to the 15th centuries; the tower, which was built between 1492 and 1524, is the latest part. The main photograph looks towards the east end and the beautiful Chapel of the Nine Altars, a very fine example of Early English style with its tall, narrow lancet windows. Henry VIII sold Fountains to Sir Richard Gresham in 1540. Although some 70 years later Sir Stephen Proctor used abbey stone to build Fountains Hall, the glorious Cistercian abbey is remarkably well preserved, a delightful medley of lichen-covered ruins which are highly impressive and preserve the plan of this great monastery almost intact. At the time when these photographs were taken, visitors to Ripon could hire a carriage to take them on the six-mile round trip to Fountains Abbey; or, if they were feeling energetic enough, they could enjoy a promenade through the woods to reach it.

A visit to Fountains is a double pleasure, for as well as the abbey there is an exceptional landscape garden to enjoy (7391, opposite, below). The Studley Royal Estate close by was inherited by John Aislabie in 1693. As a principal sponsor of the South Sea Company, he was expelled from Parliament in 1721 when the South Sea Bubble burst, and he devoted himself to creating the garden until his death in 1742. His son William continued his work; he bought the abbey ruins in 1767 and incorporated them into the garden. The serene Water Garden we see here, with its symmetrical stretches of water, and classical temple and statues, is surrounded by twisting paths through the woods, which pass various temples and follies. From one of these, Anne Boleyn's seat, the famous surprise view looks down the valley to the abbey ruins. This is one of the earliest examples of the picturesque style in England, and a masterpiece of landscape gardening.

Above:
FOUNTAINS ABBEY,
THE GREAT SEAL

RIEVAULX ABBEY

With the one exception of Salisbury Cathedral, in the whole kingdom — so we may, without exaggeration, assign to Rievaulx the first place amongst ruins of the same style. In picturesqueness of situation, too, Rievaulx will hold its own against the best — including even Tintern and Bolton, and had the ground on which it stands only been tidied up, to use a vulgar phrase, and such of the disjecta membra of its demolished parts as lie about been collected and put into something like order, it is difficult to imagine a more delightful bourne for a morning's journey than the precincts of this lovely ruin.

BADDELEY'S YORKSHIRE, 1902

 THE PILGRIMAGE OF GRACE

Henry VIII had much popular support for his Dissolution of the Monasteries, but not in the north of England, where many were still strong adherents of the Catholic faith. A serious revolt was led by a Yorkshire lawyer, Robert Aske, who raised an army of rebels 40,000 strong and marched on York and Doncaster (the Pilgrimage of Grace). Supported by the Archbishop of York, the rebels proclaimed that the revolt would 'extend no further than to the maintenance and defence of the faith of Christ and the deliverance of holy church, sore decayed and oppressed, and to the furtherance also of private and public matters in the realm concerning the wealth of all the king's poor subjects'. Henry VIII sent Thomas Howard, Duke of Norfolk, with an army to confront the rebels; but a sudden downpour prevented a battle, and Norfolk offered pardon for the pilgrims and their leaders and a parliament at York to discuss their grievances. However, Aske and his supporters were held responsible for another uprising at Beverley a few months later. They were arrested, tried for treason, and executed in 1537, along with the abbots of the four largest monasteries in the north. Northern England was placed under martial law, and about 250 people were hanged. There was no further serious opposition to the Dissolution.

Opposite:
RIEVAULX ABBEY
C1870 R86301

Left:
RIEVAULX ABBEY
C1867 3867

Below left:
RIEVAULX ABBEY,
TILES AND STONE
CARVING DETAIL
2004

Below right:
RIEVAULX ABBEY,
NAVE ARCADE 2004
R86701K

Lying in the tranquil Rye valley (Rievaulx is the French equivalent of Rye vale) two miles west of Hemsley, this was the first Cistercian monastery in the north of England. It was founded in 1132, a daughter house of Clairvaux; as well as leading their spiritual life, the French monks were also shrewd businessmen. They managed huge sheep flocks for the wool trade, as well as carrying out iron smelting, glass production and leather tanning – it is hard today to imagine that this tranquil site was once busy with industrial activity. After the Dissolution the land and the buildings were given to the Duncombe estate in Hemsley; in the 18th century Thomas Duncombe recognised the picturesque quality of the ruins and created the Rievaulx Terrace on the hill above, from which pleasing views could be obtained. Much of the village was built from the stone of the abbey buildings, especially the nave of the abbey church, but even so Rievaulx is probably the most complete Cistercian abbey in England. Here we see the stunningly beautiful church, rebuilt in the early 13th century and thus a fine example of the Early English style. The east end has two storeys of tall lancet windows (here obscured by rather too rampant ivy). Notice the richly moulded piers and arches, and the paired lancets of the clerestory.

WHITBY ABBEY

This atmospheric photograph (left) shows the gaunt ruins of Whitby Abbey, buffeted by all the winds that blow on the exposed promontory. This was one of the richest Benedictine houses in the north, but virtually nothing is left of the monastic buildings. Only the abbey church is left, a mute and impressive witness of what used to be.

St Hilda came to Whitby in the mid 7th century and founded the monastery whose fame spread far and wide. It was here in AD664 that the Synod of Whitby was held to resolve the differences between Celtic and Roman Christianity, particularly over the date of Easter; following the synod, the English church was unified under the Roman discipline, and the issue of the date of the Easter festival was settled. The early primitive abbey buildings disappeared from the historical record after the mid 8th century, probably destroyed by Viking invaders around AD867. It was not until the 11th century that the stone abbey was begun by Norman Benedictine monks. The abbey was altered and rebuilt over the years. Most of what remains dates from the 13th and early 14th centuries. Then the greed and rapacity of Henry VIII brought about the end of the monasteries, and the last Abbot of Whitby, Henry de Vall, was forced to surrender the abbey to the king's commissioners in December 1539. Once the lead had been taken from the roof, it was not long before the structure began to crumble, and much of the stone was taken for use elsewhere. Here and there around the town, a few monastic stones can be found in some walls and buildings. The west front largely collapsed in 1914 after a raid by German battle cruisers, which shelled Whitby and scored a hit on the abbey. The façade has since been partly rebuilt.

The charming vignette (66279, left), seen through the old abbey ruins, shows the sadly neglected state of this historic building with its grass-grown walls and tumbled masonry before it was taken over by the Ministry of Works, later known as English Heritage.

Right over the town is the ruin of Whitby Abbey ... It is a most noble ruin, of immense size, and full of beautiful and romantic bits; there is a legend that a white lady is seen in one of the windows. Between it and the town there is another church, the parish one, round which is a big graveyard, all full of tombstones. This is to my mind the nicest spot in Whitby, for it lies right over the town, and has a full view of the harbour and all up the bay to where the headland called Kettleness stretches out into the sea.

BRAM STOKER, 'DRACULA', 1897

Opposite above: WHITBY ABBEY 1897   39481

Opposite below: WHITBY, THE PARISH CHURCH FROM THE ABBEY 1913   66279

Above: WHITBY ABBEY, THE NORTH TRANSEPT C1885   18174

CAEDMON – THE FIRST ENGLISH POET

Caedmon, an illiterate labourer who worked at Whitby Abbey, was perhaps the first English poet. He was inspired to sing by a vision in which an angel appeared to him, and he told of the creation and God's world in song. When Hilda heard of his talent, she took him into the community and he became a monk, for at this time Whitby was a mixed monastery of both nuns and monks. In his 'The Ecclesiastical History of the English Nation', Bede records the song Caedmon sang for the angel, and later sang for Abbess Hilda:

'Praise we the Fashioner now of Heaven's fabric,
The majesty of his might and his mind's wisdom,
Work of the world warden, worker of all wonders,
How he the Lord of Glory everlasting,
Wrought first for the race of men
Heaven as a rooftree,
Then made he Middle Earth to be their mansion.'

Bede also tells how when he became a monk, Caedmon was 'particularly remarkable for the Grace of God, and was wont to make religious verses, so that whatever was interpreted to him out of scripture, he soon after put the same into poetical expressions of much sweetness and humility in English, which was his native language. By his verse the minds of many were often excited to despise the world, and to aspire to heaven'.

FURNESS ABBEY

... A structure famed
Beyond its neighbourhood, the antique walls
Of that large abbey which within the Vale
Of Nightshade, to St Mary's honour built,
Stands yet a mouldering pile with fractured arch,
Belfry, and images, and living trees,
A holy scene!

Through the walls we flew
And down the valley, and, a circuit made
In wantonness of heart, through rough and smooth
We scampered homeward.

WILLIAM WORDSWORTH,
FROM 'THE PRELUDE', 1805

Left:
FURNESS ABBEY 1892
30569

Below left:
FURNESS ABBEY,
NORMAN ARCHES
1892   30580

In 1127, England's future King Stephen, whilst still Earl of Moreton and Boulogne, founded Furness Abbey in 'the Vale of Deadly Nightshade'. The abbey (dedicated to the Virgin Mary) grew, and eventually owned lands in Ireland and the Isle of Man. It founded daughter houses at Swineshead on the east coast and Saddell on the Kintyre peninsula in Scotland. Furness became the second richest Cistercian monastery in England, second only to Fountains Abbey.

The monks had several granges, or farms, in the area (the word comes from the French for granary). They also had the fishing rights of Beaumont Fishery in Lancashire. Whilst the monks, known as choir monks, attended to the religious affairs of the abbey, most of the physical work was done by lay brothers. In 1332 Robert the Bruce attacked Furness and was entertained at the abbey by the abbot, John Cockerham, who paid a ransom for the district not to be plundered. In 1537 the abbey was surrendered to Henry VIII – it was the first major monastery to be dissolved. Until its dissolution, Furness Abbey had dominated the local economy. For many years after the dissolution the site was in the ownership of the Preston family; it passed on to the Cavendishes, and finally to English Heritage.

The arches shown in 30580 (below) are an example of the earliest Norman period of the abbey.

Birds of the present generation are the posterity of those who first settled in the ruins, after the Reformation, and perhaps the old monks of a still earlier day may have watched them building about the abbey, before it was a ruin at all ...   NATHANIEL HAWTHORNE, 1855

The view of this stately mass, 'half church of God, half castle against the Scots', from the viaduct and railway station high on the opposite western slope of the river, is one of surpassing grandeur; the most magnificent embodiment in stone and mortar of the old English idea of Church and State which our island affords ... When we have entered the church, and look down the nave, we must admit that no grander Norman building exists. It is homogeneously majestic in its wondrous solemnity. 'Look at the perfect symmetry of the great arcades, of choir and nave: the pillars are neither too short and broad, nor are they again too lofty and slender, but are admirably adapted to carry out the proportions of the whole'.

H B TRISTRAM, 1884

DURHAM CATHEDRAL FROM THE RIVER 1921   70712T

Durham is regarded by many as being the cradle of Christianity in England. It was the resting place of the precious body of St Cuthbert, who died in AD687; his remains were so venerated that when the Vikings sacked Lindisfarne the monks left the island to seek a safe sanctuary for their relics. In AD995, after years of wandering the north, the guardians of St Cuthbert's coffin came to a place called Dun Holm, the future Durham. In AD999 an Anglo-Saxon minster was built, which became a place of pilgrimage as miracles attributed to St Cuthbert became well known. Among the early pilgrims was King Canute.

When William the Conqueror finally took control of Durham, he combined the powers of the bishop and the Earl of Northumbria to create Durham's first prince bishop, a Norman called William Walcher. Walcher's leadership was weak, which ultimately resulted in his being murdered at Gateshead in 1081. His replacement was William St Carileph, the man responsible for building the present cathedral, which occupies the site of the old minster. Carileph began its construction in 1093. He designed the greater part of the cathedral as it stands today; the new building was completed to the bishop's designs in around forty years. Unfortunately, Carileph did not live to see the completion of his cathedral in 1135.

DURHAM CATHEDRAL

 DURHAM'S SANCTUARY
KNOCKER

*The grimacing head of the
sanctuary knocker is hardly
a welcoming sight for visitors
or those seeking refuge in the
cathedral. It represents the right
of sanctuary for fugitives, who
could find temporary shelter
in the cathedral from their*

*pursuers. The right of sanctuary can be traced back to
AD597. Later Saxon laws gave these special privileges to
St Cuthbert's community in around AD900. The Normans
continued to observe the tradition, and at Durham
sanctuary was granted for 37 days. The Galilee bell was
tolled to inform everyone that a fugitive was present; he
would only be admitted if he had no weapons. He would
be given food and drink and made to wear a black
gown with a large yellow cross of St Cuthbert on the
left shoulder. In fact, it was not really necessary for the
pursued to enter the cathedral, because the boundaries
of sanctuary at Durham probably extended as far as
Neville's Cross and Gillesgate. A replica knocker now
replaces the original, which can be seen in the Treasures
of St Cuthbert exhibition in the cathedral.*

Previous page, below: DURHAM
CATHEDRAL, THE MEMORIAL CHAPEL
1925 77671

Above left: DURHAM CATHEDRAL,
THE CRYPT C1862 1119

Top: DURHAM CATHEDRAL,
ST CUTHBERT'S CROSS

Above: DURHAM CATHEDRAL,
THE GALILEE

The work of building the cathedral
can be attributed to several distinct
periods. The nave, transepts and
the four west choir bays were built
between 1093 and 1133; Bishop
Pudsey added the Galilee Chapel at
the western end in 1175; the two west
towers were built between 1217 and
1226; then the east end of the choir
was altered and the Chapel of the Nine
Altars erected between 1242 and 1280.
The great central tower was rebuilt
between 1465 and 1495 after lightning
had destroyed its predecessor some
60 years earlier. The sheer size of the
magnificent structure is awesome: the
central tower soars to a phenomenal
218 feet and has 325 steps, should we
wish to tackle the ascent. The entire
building stretches 470 feet from the
east wall of the Chapel of the Nine
Altars to the west wall of the Galilee
Chapel, and the great nave runs for
201 feet, its roof rising some 72 feet.

The crypt (1119, above left) is one
of the oldest parts of the cathedral,
and is now used to house the Treasures
of St Cuthbert exhibition and the
cathedral restaurant. Most visitors to
the cathedral use the cloisters to gain
access to the restaurant, the bookshop
and the Treasury Museum, one of
the most important museums in the
north of England.

The Memorial Chapel (77671,
previous page) was dedicated in 1924
to commemorate Durham's own
regiment, the Durham Light Infantry.
It contains the regimental colours and
books of remembrance listing the
names of those who fell in battle.

TINTERN ABBEY

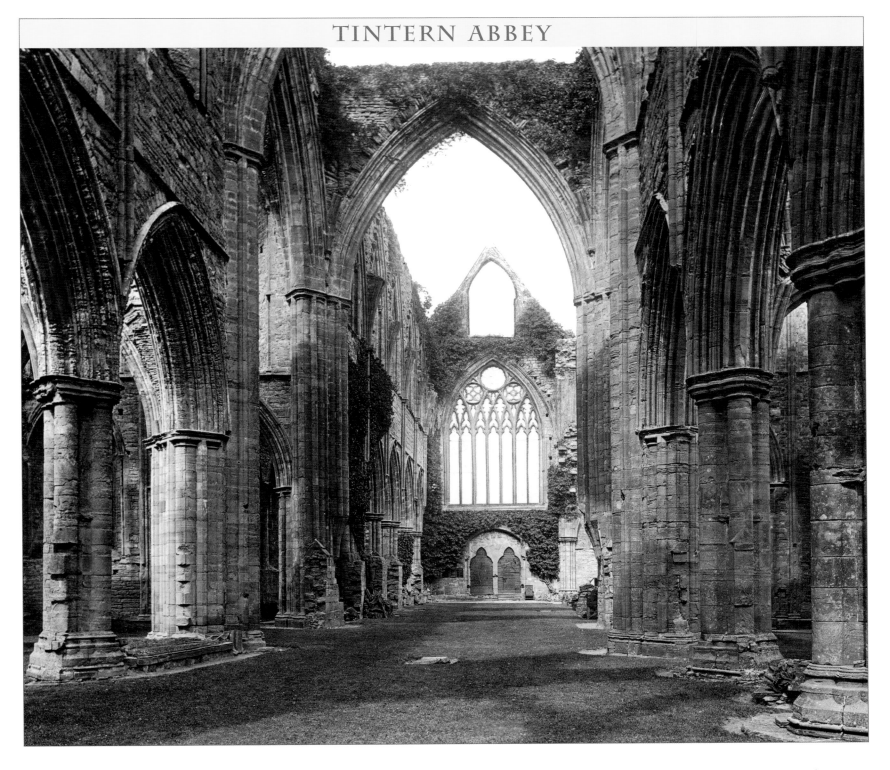

TINTERN ABBEY, THE NAVE LOOKING WEST 1893   32476

We have this evening got into a nook for which I would give all the Welch mountains grand as they are & if you and Mrs Richmond could but spare a week you might see Tintern & be back again … I think of the Abbey – & such an Abbey! the lightest Gothic – trellised with ivy & rising from a wilderness of orchards – & set like a gem amongst the folding of woody hills.

SAMUEL PALMER, 1835, FROM A LETTER TO GEORGE RICHMOND

The Cistercian Tintern Abbey was founded in 1131 by Walter de la Clare. The first brothers of the establishment came directly from Normandy. The remains to be seen today actually date from the abbey's rebuilding in the course of the 13th to the 15th centuries. The abbey's primary occupation was agriculture, and it reached the apogee of its wealth and influence in the 14th century, when it was reckoned the wealthiest abbey in Wales. The Dissolution of the Monasteries in the 1530s brought the inevitable decline and subsequent neglect of its fabric. Lead from the roof was stripped (to be re-used at Raglan and Chepstow castles), and the ivy-clad ruins were later to become a focus for the romantic travellers of the 18th and 19th centuries, notably the poet Wordsworth and the painter Turner. The total length of the church is 228 feet; the nave has six bays, the choir four, and the transepts three. In Victorian times it was possible to climb the structure and walk along the top of the principal walls: 'To anyone with a steady head there is not the slightest risk, and the views which this elevated station commands are exceedingly beautiful'. Today, it is likely that such an undertaking would be frowned upon by Cadw, the custodians of the abbey and its grounds!

The haunting photograph 32476 (previous page) shows the deep mouldings and intricate architectural details of the abbey. The central area would have been used as the lay brothers' choir, and a screen wall would have divided off the aisles at the north and south. The doors in the bottom of the far wall are no longer in place.

Above:
TINTERN ABBEY C1872 6358

Right:
TINTERN ABBEY 2004 T53701

We crossed a field and the fold of a farm house, scrambled down a narrow stony lane and struck the main road again. About a mile above Llanthony we descried the Abbey ruins, the dim grey pile of building in the vale below standing by the little river side among its brilliant green meadow. What was our horror on entering the enclosure to see two tourists with staves and shoulder belts all complete postured among the ruins in an attitude of admiration, one of them of course discoursing learnedly to his gaping companion and pointing out objects of interest with his stick. If there is one thing more hateful than another it is being told what to admire and having objects pointed out to one with a stick. Of all noxious animals too the most noxious is a tourist.

FRANCIS KILVERT, 1870

LLANTHONY PRIORY

The tranquillity of the Vale of Ewyas and its surrounding hills must have appealed to the Augustinian monks who founded a church here in 1108, possibly on a site where St David, the patron saint of Wales, had lived centuries earlier. Its Welsh name is Llanddewi Nant Honddu, meaning 'the church of St David on the Honddu brook'. The abbey has suffered from Welsh uprisings against the Normans and the English; soon after it was built, it was abandoned for almost fifty years, and the Owain Glyndwr uprising in the 15th century did not leave it unscathed. By the Dissolution, it had dwindled to a prior and four canons. The priory itself, built at various times between 1180 and 1230, is in ruins, yet its magnificent setting remains a place for peaceful contemplation. The poet Walter Savage Landor owned the abbey ruins in the early 19th century; he had hoped to transform the lands and the estate, but was foiled by the uncooperative locals. He wrote, perhaps ironically, of Llanthony:

'I loved thee by thy streams of yore,
By distant streams I love thee more.'

Above: LLANTHONY PRIORY, FROM THE NORTH-WEST 1893 32614P

MONASTERY OFFICIALS: 2

The refectorian was in charge of the frater, or refectory: he had to supply and take care of its furniture, tablecloths, napkins, and dishes, and he had to renew the rushes on the floor five times a year. He also had to provide clean water and clean towels for the lavatorium, or wash basin, in the cloister – and it was his duty to sample the cheeses for the community. The kitchener presided over the cooks, and was in charge of the larders and the kitchen utensils. The infirmarian looked after the old and the sick; one monastery rule book says that he had to be 'gentle, and good-tempered, kind, compassionate to the sick, and willing as far as possible to gratify their needs with affectionate sympathy'. The infirmarian also performed blood-letting, an operation which was recommended for all the monks four times a year. Other officials included the almoner, who distributed alms to the poor; the chamberlain, who took care of the monks' clothes and bedclothes; and the master of novices, who trained the novice monks.

BRECON PRIORY

When Bernard de Neufmarche established the Norman Lordship of Brecknock in 1093 he endowed a Benedictine cell in Brecon. The priory stood to the north-east of Brecon Castle on the site of the church of St John the Evangelist. The Norman church was probably similar in size and shape to the present building. All that remains of this early church is the font and stonework at the east end of the nave. The font is carved with grotesque masks with birds and beasts entwined in a style typical of the Norman period. The church was rebuilt first in around 1201; then by the end of the 14th century two chapels were added. In those days plastered walls would have been covered in colourful paintings, and the aisles would have been portioned and occupied by chantry chapels of the craft guilds in the borough. A screen across the nave at the chancel arch would have formed a boundary between the parochial and the monastic areas of worship, with the parish altar on the nave side. Above the screen would have been the rood, a striking representation of the Crucifixion. The golden cross was believed to have healing properties, and it was so esteemed by pilgrims that the church became known as the church of the Holy Rood, or Holy Cross.

Above right: BRECON, THE PRIORY CHURCH 1899 44726

At the time of its dissolution the priory community consisted of a prior, four monks and fifteen servants. The church was saved from destruction because it was used as a parish church. However, the rood and many of the medieval treasures were destroyed. A rare cresset stone with 30 cups hollowed out to blaze with lights used to sit near the door of the church, but it is now on display in the Heritage Centre. In 1923 the priory church of St John the Evangelist became the cathedral church of the new diocese of Swansea and Brecon.

LLANDAFF CATHEDRAL

When the present Bishop of Llandaff presented himself at the cathedral to demand installation into his sacred office [1850], the western portion of the building, through which the procession had to pass, was, as it had been for 127 years, a roofless ruin. The beautiful window in the western facade was dilapidated and unglazed. A lofty fragment of what had once been a south-west tower frowned haughtily upon the desolation below, threatening at any moment still further destruction. Thick branches of ivy had forced themselves into the joints of the noble columns of the arches which had so long been exposed to wind and weather.

E A FISHBOURNE, 1884

Left: LLANDAFF CATHEDRAL, THE WEST FRONT 1893 32701
Above: LLANDAFF CATHEDRAL, THE NAVE LOOKING WEST 1893 32704

Llandaff, whose name means 'the sacred enclosure on the River Taff', is just two miles north of Cardiff. The cathedral is one of the earliest ecclesiastical foundations in Britain. Like all of the earliest churches, little remains of the original; as it passed through the next 1,500 years, it endured changes in every historical period. A new west front was built in about 1220. This west front is judged to be amongst the best works of art in Wales. In the 13th century the chapter house was built, and before the century ended the Lady Chapel was added. The cathedral suffered neglect during the Reformation, but the 19th century saw a splendid transformation when the cathedral was restored to its earlier glory. The restoration was only temporary, however, for in 1941 the cathedral was all but wrecked by a German landmine. Among British cathedrals, only Coventry suffered worse damage. Some old treasures survived the blitz, including Rossetti's triptych 'The Seed of David'.

In the 6th century, St Dyfrig founded the cathedral close to the River Taff. He was succeeded by St Teilo, and then by Teilo's nephew, Euddogwy. These three Celtic saints remain the patron saints of the present cathedral, and are represented by the carving known as the three faces and four eyes.

In the 19th century, restoration work was undertaken by Prichard & Partners. A new clerestory was added, ruined arcades were renewed, and an open timbered roof was constructed over the nave (see 32704, previous page). Prichard's work proved controversial amongst his peers. Leading 'medievalist' architects and devotees, including William Burges, were unimpressed and quick to voice their misgivings in print. Today, following the damage of the Second World War, the interior of the cathedral is totally different. A bold arch by the architect George Pace now spans the nave, carrying Sir Jacob Epstein's aluminium figure of Christ in Majesty (L67165, right); it stands between the nave and the choir, and without interrupting it, breaks the view of the whole building from the top of the steps inside the west door.

Above left:
LLANDAFF
CATHEDRAL,
THE SOUTH DOOR
C1874   7040

Above right:
LLANDAFF
CATHEDRAL,
A CAPITAL – THREE
FACES AND FOUR EYES
C1955   L67046

Left:
LLANDAFF
CATHEDRAL,
EPSTEIN'S MAJESTAS
C1960   L67165

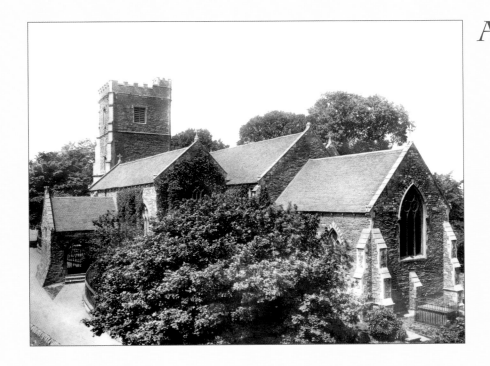

According to tradition, the local area west of the Usk was ruled in the 6th century by a king called Gwynllyw. He had a reputation as a robber and a thief, but he was persuaded to repent of his ways by Tathan, an Irish hermit, and decided to build a church on Stow Hill. One day he found a white ox with a black spot on his forehead, and took this to be an omen that this was the site where he should build the church. The church is now the cathedral church of St Woolos – the name Woolos is a corruption of the name Gwynllyw. The church we see today is largely Norman work, built at the time when Robert FitzHamon founded the castle in 1171. In 1921, with the disestablishment of the Church in Wales, the diocese of Monmouth was created out of the diocese of Llandaff. St Woolos's Church, the medieval parish church of Newport, was declared its pro-cathedral. The town's prestige was enhanced when the church was granted full cathedral status in 1949.

Below left (N25121) we see the noble Norman nave arcade with its plain arches and scallop-topped capitals. Between 1961 and 1962 a new chancel was built to replace the Victorian one. This features the work of the artist John Piper: a large abstract mural and window behind the high altar.

An unusual feature of the cathedral is its Galilee Chapel between the tower and the nave (N25120, below). This doorway leads to the nave; the arch with its typically Norman ornamental carving is flanked by two columns, which appear to be Roman – they are said to have been brought from Caerleon, the Roman Isca.

Above left:
NEWPORT,
THE CHURCH OF
ST WOOLOS 1899   43663

Below left:
NEWPORT,
ST WOOLOS'S
CATHEDRAL,
THE INTERIOR 1932
N25121

Right:
NEWPORT,
ST WOOLOS'S
CATHEDRAL,
THE INTERIOR 1932
N25120

NEWPORT, ST WOOLOS'S CATHEDRAL

NEATH ABBEY

Neath Abbey, founded in 1130, was originally a Savigniac foundation, but it became Cistercian in 1147. The west range, where the lay brothers lived, dates from the 12th century, and the rest mostly from the 13th. After the Dissolution in 1539, the abbot's house was converted into a mansion by Sir John Herbert. Copper smelting was carried out in the area, and by the 17th century the abbey ruins themselves were being used as a smelting works, with workmen living in the by now dilapidated mansion. Later still, the abbey was surrounded by a canal and a railway line, and the ruins were buried under industrial waste – a dreadful fate for the once beautiful abbey. However, in the 1920s and 30s it was cleared, and was taken into state ownership in the 1940s; the ruins and their setting are now restored.

Top: NEATH ABBEY 1893   32725A

Above: NEATH ABBEY 1893   32725B

HEAD SHAVING

The brother who undertook the office of barber kept his implements– razors, strop, soap, and brushes, etc – in a small movable chest, which usually stood near the dormitory door. When necessary he carried it down to the cloister, where, at any time that the community were at work or sitting in the cloister, he could sharpen up his razors or prepare his soaps. When the time of the general 'rasura' came, the community sat silently in two lines, one set along the cloister wall, the other facing them with their backs to the windows. The general shaving was made a religious act, like almost every other incident of cloister life, by the recitation of psalms. The brothers who shaved the others, and those who carried the dishes and

razors, were directed to say the 'Benedicite' together before beginning their work; all the rest as they sat there during the ceremony, except of course the individual actually being operated upon, said the 'Verba mea' and other psalms. It would seem that the usual interval between the times of shaving the monks' tonsures was about three weeks.

ABBOT GASQUET, 1904

ST DAVIDS CATHEDRAL

A steep lane paved with rounded stones leads down to the Tower Gate ... A few steps more and the first extended view of the cathedral buildings is gained. The spectator looks down on them nestling in the narrow green valley of the Alan, while beyond the stream rises the fine bishop's palace (now in ruins), backed by the crags of Carn Llidi and St David's Head itself. It is a most striking scene, and grows on one more and more every time one sees it.

W A B COOLIDGE, 1884

Above: ST DAVIDS CATHEDRAL, FROM THE SOUTH WEST 1890   27908

Left: ST DAVIDS, THE BISHOP'S PALACE, ST MARY'S CHAPEL 1890   27920

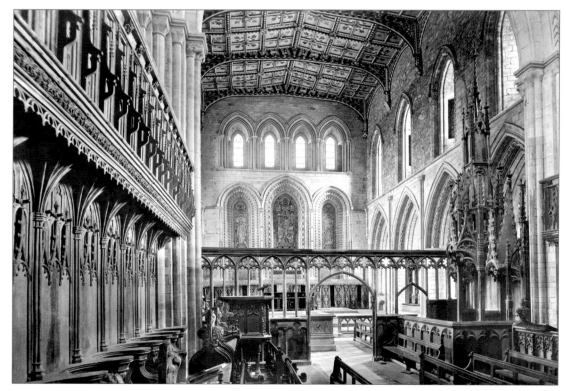

St Davids, or Tyddewi, is named after Dewi Sant, the patron saint of Wales (he died on 1 March AD588) who established his monastery here on the banks of the River Alun.

The legend has it that David, about to speak to an assembled crowd, was concerned they would not be able to see him. He dropped his handkerchief onto the ground, which sank down, forming a hollow, a natural amphitheatre in which everyone could see and hear him. The cathedral was built on this spot. However, it is more likely that the cathedral was built in a hollow so as to escape the attention of marauding Vikings. The atmospheric cathedral complex, through which the little river runs, includes the well-preserved remains of the impressive Bishop's Palace; all was once surrounded by a curtain wall – the Norman response to its having been attacked and pillaged at least eight times.

The city of St Davids (the smallest city in Britain – it is not much more than a village) stands in a somewhat austere location in the far west of Wales on a windswept plateau, but the cathedral itself is sheltered in its hollow. The interior of the cathedral is simply stunning. The roof beams were renewed in the 19th century (27915, below left). The bishop's throne, dating from c1500, is on the right in front of the open wooden screen which separates the choir from the presbytery. The tomb beyond the screen is that of Edmund Tudor, Earl of Richmond, the father of the first Tudor monarch Henry VII. William the Conqueror once journeyed here to pray in this well-known place of pilgrimage – two pilgrimages to St David's was considered equal to a pilgrimage to Rome.

St Mary's Chapel (27920, previous page) is in the remains of the extensive Bishop's Palace, which is now much restored.

Above left:
DRAWING OF ST DAVIDS CATHEDRAL, THE TIMBER ROOF
Above right:
ST DAVIDS CATHEDRAL AND THE CLOSE 2003
S14701K
Left:
ST DAVIDS CATHEDRAL, THE CHOIR
LOOKING EAST 1890 27915

STRATA FLORIDA ABBEY

Strata Florida was originally established in this remote spot by the Normans in 1163, but when Lord Rhys took control of most of Ceredigion he re-established the abbey on a new site, where Cistercian monks spent about 50 years building one of the first stone buildings in the county. The abbey was dissolved by Henry VIII in 1539 and was sold to the Earl of Essex and his agent, John Stedman, whose family later used much of the stone in their mansion and farm buildings. This photograph shows the great west door of the abbey church. Built in the early 13th century, it is an unusual design: the jambs run uninterrupted in one continuous arch, seemingly bound together with ring mouldings.

Left: PONTRHYDFENDIGAID, STRATA FLORIDA ABBEY C1950 P211010

BANGOR CATHEDRAL

The first monastic settlement was founded here by St Deiniol in about AD525, some 70 years before St Augustine arrived in Canterbury. Deiniol was given the land, probably by Maelgwn, King of Gwynedd; he enclosed it with a wattle fence, a 'bangor' (hence the name of the town), and within this enclosure Deiniol and his followers built a church and huts to live in. The site was much fought over. The Vikings destroyed the first cathedral, and in the 12th century it was rebuilt, only to be destroyed again; conflicts between the English and the Welsh, including the revolt of Owain Glyndwr, meant that the cathedral was repeatedly damaged and repaired between the 13th and the 16th century, when the nave with its six arches and the western tower were built.

Right:
BANGOR,
ST DEINIOL'S
CATHEDRAL
1906   54822P

The cathedral was restored by Sir George Gilbert Scott in the 1870s. Scott partially reconstructed the choir, transepts and chapter house 'in such a style as is indicated by their few remaining fragments'. There was not enough money for Scott to build more than a stump of a tower; when money became available to complete Scott's scheme in the 1950s, a spire could not be built, owing to subsidence. In the late 1960s the tower was finished off with battlements, a pyramidal roof and a weathercock. Three princes of Gwynedd are buried here, and there is a memorial to the poet Goronwy Owen, who left to teach in America in the 18th century.

ST ASAPH CATHEDRAL

The cathedral of St Asaph dominates this view of the town, which stands between the Clwyd and Elwy rivers. Legend tells that St Kentigern, Bishop of Strathclyde, was driven into exile and founded a monastery here; when he returned to Scotland in about AD573, St Asaph succeeded him. Many place names in this area commemorating St Asaph suggest that the monastery was an influential one, and when the Normans reached this part of Wales, they built a new cathedral church in which the relics of St Asaph were enshrined. The 13th century was one of war between the Welsh and the English, and the cathedral was damaged, and set on fire by English soldiers. Between 1284 and 1392, the cathedral was largely rebuilt in sandstone; to raise the necessary money, pilgrims were encouraged to visit the shrine of St Asaph and give alms. However, in 1402 the rebel Owain Glyndwr sacked and burnt the new cathedral; it was not until the end of the 15th century that the building was fully repaired. Just before this photograph was taken, Sir George Gilbert Scott had restored the cathedral.

Above left: ST ASAPH, FROM THE RIVER 1890   23295

The Abbey has been built of a pale red stone; that part which was first erected of a very durable kind, the sculptured flowers and leaves and other minute ornaments being as perfect in many places as when first wrought. The ruin is of considerable extent, but unfortunately it is almost surrounded by insignificant houses, so that when you are close to it you see it entirely separated from many rural objects, and even when viewed from a distance the situation does not seem to be particularly happy, for the vale is broken and disturbed, and the Abbey at a distance from the river, so that you do not look upon them as companions of each other. And surely this is a national barbarism: within these beautiful walls is the ugliest church that was ever beheld — if it had been hewn out of the side of a hill it could not have been more dismal; there was no neatness, nor even decency, and it appeared to be so damp and so completely excluded from fresh air, that it must be dangerous to sit in it. What a contrast to the beautiful and graceful order apparent in every part of the ancient design and workmanship!

DOROTHY WORDSWORTH, 1803

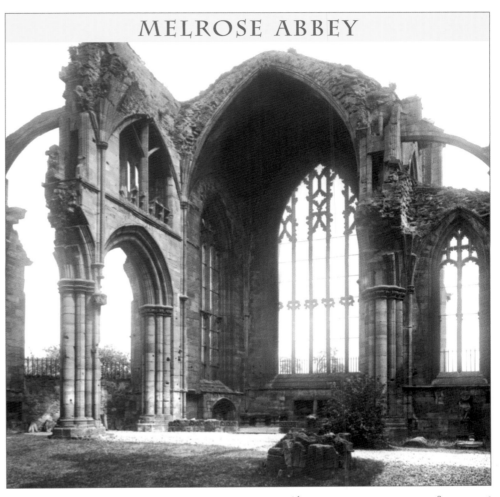

Above: MELROSE ABBEY 1897   39196

Acommunity was founded at Melrose by St Aidan cAD660, on a site about four miles from the present abbey. St Cuthbert lived there before becoming Prior of Lindisfarne in AD664. Later, David I encouraged Cistercian monks sent by Bernard of Clairvaux to found a new abbey on the present site, which was dedicated in 1146. Like all the abbeys in the Borders, Melrose suffered from the conflicts between Scotland and England throughout the Middle Ages. In 1385, Melrose was one of the places sacked by the forces of the English king, Richard II, which 'saved nothing and burnt down with fiery flames God's temples and holy places – to wit the monasteries of Melrose, Dryburgh and Newbattle'. The monks rebuilt the abbey after the raid, and it is the ruins of this rebuild that we see today. The grandeur of the late Decorated and early Perpendicular architecture is very unlike the austere style that the Cistercians normally used, but by this time the order had become less strict – these ruins are among the most glorious in Britain. Much fine flowing window tracery survives, and also much ornamental carving, including gargoyles and a depiction of the coronation of the Virgin.

SIR WALTER SCOTT

The popular and hugely influential author Sir Walter Scott was buried beside his ancestors in the chapel in the north transept in 1832. His home, Abbotsford, was close by, and 'Scott's View' is a viewpoint above the abbey that he visited regularly. Born in Edinburgh, Scott grew to love the Scottish Borders when as a boy he was sent to his grandfather's farm in Tweedale to recuperate after the attack of polio which lamed him for life. Indeed, his first major work was 'The Minstrelsy of the Scottish Border' (1802-03), Border ballads collected (and sometimes 'improved') by Scott. He began to build Abbotsford in 1811, and worked seemingly tirelessly here and in Edinburgh on his famous novels, including 'The Bride of Lammermoor', 'Rob Roy', and 'Ivanhoe'. He died at Abbotsford soon after his return from a tour of the Mediterranean.

Above: DRYBURGH ABBEY, SIR WALTER SCOTT'S TOMB 1897   39201

After breakfast we set out in the rain to the ruins of Dryburgh Abbey ... We rang a bell at the gate, and, instead of a porter, an old woman came to open it through a narrow side-alley cut in a thick plantation of evergreens. On entering, saw the thatch of her hut just above the trees, and it looked very pretty, but the poor creature herself was a figure to frighten a child, – bowed almost double, having a hooked nose and overhanging eyebrows, a complexion stained brown with smoke, and a cap that might have been worn for months and never washed. No doubt she had been cowering over her peat fire, for if she had emitted smoke by her breath and through every pore, the odour could not have been stronger. This ancient woman, by right of office, attended us to show off the curiosities, and she had her tale as perfect ... The house of Lord Buchan and the Abbey stand upon a large flat peninsula, a green holm almost covered with fruit-trees. The ruins of Dryburgh are much less extensive than those of Melrose, and greatly inferior both in the architecture and stone, which is much mouldered away. Lord Buchan has trained pear-trees along the walls, which are bordered with flowers and gravel walks, and he has made a pigeon-house, and a fine room in the ruin, ornamented with a curiously-assorted collection of busts of eminent men, in which lately a ball was given ...

DOROTHY WORDSWORTH, 1803

DRYBURGH ABBEY

Dryburgh sits in a fine location in a loop of the River Tweed. The first Premonstratensian house in Scotland, it was founded in 1150 by Hugh de Moreville, Constable of Scotland, who later entered the abbey himself as a novice, and spent the rest of his life in the abbey he had created. The White Canons followed the rule of St Augustine, and observed the rule of silence. The building was damaged by English forces several times; after one raid in 1322, King Robert the Bruce, among others, contributed towards rebuilding. After a worse raid in 1385, most of the west end of the church had to be rebuilt, and the building was altered and extended throughout the 15th century. Some of the claustral buildings remain, including the chapter house and the warming room, where the monks could enjoy the warmth of a fire before returning to their tasks in unheated rooms.

Above: DRYBURGH ABBEY 1897   39199

WAKING IN THE SMALL HOURS

At some short time before the hour appointed for the commencement of the night Office the signal for rising was given in the common dormitory … It was the duty of one of the novices to light candles for his fellows, and set them about the places they occupied in the choir, since they did not as yet know the psalmody by heart. Meanwhile the monks when roused from their sleep were taught to begin the day by signing themselves with the cross and commending themselves to God's protection. As they rose from their beds they put on those parts of their monastic habit which had been laid aside during the hours of sleep, and shod themselves with their 'night-boots'. These were probably fur-lined, cloth protectors for the feet, which served the double purpose of keeping them warm during the winter nights spent in the cold church, and of rendering their footfall inaudible, during the hours of the greater silence which lasted from Compline till Prime. Each monk as he finished his simple preparation, seated himself in front of his bed and there waited in silence, with his hood drawn well over his head, till the bell began to toll. Then, preceded by a junior carrying a lighted lantern, the religious went out of the dormitory in companies of six at a time, and took their places in the choir.

ABBOT GASQUET, 1904

GLASGOW CATHEDRAL

Founded in 1136, on the site of St Mungo's (St Kentigern's) Church of the 6th century, the cathedral has gone through many times of peace and strife. On one door in the cathedral lead shot can still be seen; it bears witness to the citizens' successful defence against the Reformation zealots who would have destroyed it – it is probably the only one of Scotland's cathedrals to survive the Reformation of the 1560s unscathed. The affection of the ordinary people and tradesmen of Glasgow for their cathedral kept it safe. St Mungo (St Kentigern), Bishop of Strathclyde, founded a church on this site cAD590 and was buried here – today, his tomb is in the lower choir. The first stone church was consecrated in 1136, but was destroyed soon afterwards, and Bishop Jocelyn consecrated a new church in 1197; the lower walls of the nave date from this time. Much of the rest of the building belongs to the 1200s, in particular the upper and lower choirs: the cathedral stands on a sloping site, so there is room for a beautiful vaulted lower choir under the upper one. The crossing tower (and two western towers, removed in the 19th century) was built in the 1400s.

The upper part of the nave with its timbered ceiling was completed in 1480. Photograph 39779 (above left) shows the screen, or pulpitum, separating the nave and choir; the photograph also conveys the feeling of spaciousness in the cathedral, even though the building is not actually very large, about 285 feet long by 63 feet wide. The impression of height (the nave is 105 feet high) is enhanced by the narrow proportions of the nave and choir, and by the short transepts. Notice the elegant lancet windows at the east end.

Photograph 39778 (below left) shows the view from the choir towards the nave and the magnificent window at the west end. During the 19th century the windows throughout the church were filled with stained glass, most of it from Munich, at a cost close to £100,000.

Opposite: GLASGOW CATHEDRAL 1897 39772

Above left: GLASGOW CATHEDRAL, THE CHOIR LOOKING WEST 1897 39779

Below left: GLASGOW CATHEDRAL, THE NAVE LOOKING EAST 1897 39778

EDINBURGH, ST GILES'S CATHEDRAL

The present High Kirk of St Giles is usually referred to as St Giles's Cathedral. The tower, which dates from c1495, is topped off with what is considered to be the finest example of a crown steeple in the whole of Scotland. In 1634 Charles I attempted to re-establish the Scottish Episcopal Church, and St Giles's was for a short period elevated to the status of a cathedral. It became a cathedral again under Charles II, only to revert to being a parish church in 1688.

The oldest parish church in Edinburgh, much of St Giles's was badly damaged by fire in 1385, and the rebuilding was not completed until 1460. During the Reformation the interior of the church was defaced, and altars and relics were destroyed. In 1559 John Knox was appointed minister of St Giles's. The building was in fact divided into four separate churches, and remained so until the 19th century.

In 1644 James Graham, 5th Earl of Montrose, raised an army to fight for Charles I. Against all odds, Montrose gained victory after victory until his luck finally ran out at Philliphaugh in September 1645. Montrose escaped to the Continent, but returned to raise troops for Charles II. Betrayed to the Covenanters, he was hanged, drawn and quartered at Edinburgh on 21 May 1650. His tomb is shown in 39130 (left).

Opposite:
EDINBURGH,
ST GILES'S CATHEDRAL
1897   39126

Above left:
EDINBURGH,
ST GILES'S CATHEDRAL,
THE TOMB OF THE
MARQUESS OF
MONTROSE 1897   39130

Below left:
EDINBURGH,
ST GILES'S CATHEDRAL,
THE CHOIR
LOOKING WEST 1897
39129

INCHCOLM ABBEY

The ruins of Inchcolm Abbey, 'the Iona of the East', are amongst the best preserved monastic buildings in Scotland, fulfilling the wish on a medieval Latin inscription above one of the abbey doorways: 'Stet domus haec donec fluctus formica marinos ebibat, et totum testudo perambulet orbem' – 'May this house stand until an ant drains the flowing sea, and a tortoise walks around the whole world'. Inchcolm is a tiny island in the Firth of Forth just off the coast of Fife. Here in 1123 Alexander I took refuge – he was crossing the Forth when a storm came up – and was tended by a hermit, whose ancient cell still stands close to the abbey. In gratitude, the king vowed to found an abbey dedicated to St Columba; however, his death the following year meant that the abbey was built by his successor David I. The abbey as we see it today was built at different times, with the abbey church itself the oldest part. The cloisters are most unusual in that they are not a covered walk, but form the ground floor of the abbey buildings. In the refectory we can see the remains of the pulpit where a monk read to his companions while they ate. Inchcolm was attacked by the English many times in the 14th century, and appears to have been deserted just before the Reformation.

The chapter house (45924, left) probably dates from the 13th century. It is octagonal, with small windows, a fine doorway, and a groined vault supported by round pillars. At the centre of the roof a round hole opens into the floor of a room above; the hole may have been used for raising and lowering a lamp. The room above the chapter house was probably a warming room or study for the monks. The tradition is that this room was built by the Scots historian Walter Bower as his personal study. He was the eleventh abbot, whose reign began in 1418; we can picture him, or his monks, keeping warm here while the sea lashed around the lonely island.

Above left: INCHCOLM ABBEY 1900   45921

Below left: INCHCOLM ABBEY,
THE NORMAN ARCH AND THE CHAPTER
HOUSE 1900   45924

The portion of the cathedral where public worship is held is walled out of the old building in an arbitrary ugly fashion. It is very plain inside, and down below intensely cold. We generally sit in the west gallery, the high old pews distressingly covered with hieroglyphics. They are open under the seat, and non nunquam descends a peppermint, hop, hop, hop, from tier to tier. One looks down on the dusty tops of the sounding-board, a rickety canopy carved somewhat to resemble the crown of St Giles Cathedral [in Edinburgh], but its effect is marred by being tipped forward as though it might fall on Mr Rutherford, earnest, pale and foxy-haired, with a pointed beard and decent Geneva bands.

BEATRIX POTTER, 1892

Dunkeld stands on one of the main routes from the Lowlands to the Highlands, at the point where the River Braan meets the River Tay. Celtic missionaries, known as Culdees, established the first monastery here. The cathedral is dedicated to St Columba. In the 9th century, Kenneth MacAlpin, the first king of the united Scots and Picts, made Dunkeld the religious centre of Scotland, and the relics of St Columba were moved here from Iona for safety. The cathedral whose remains we see today was begun in 1325, and shows both Gothic and Norman influences. It remained an important ecclesiastical centre until the Reformation, when it was mostly pulled down; the choir, which dates from the mid 14th century, was re-roofed in 1600 and became the parish church. Although Dunkeld became a thriving market town after the Reformation, its wealth and importance had declined by Victorian times, and much of the area round the cathedral became ruinous. However, the National Trust for Scotland and the local council began a vigorous restoration programme, and today the cathedral and the town look much as they must have done before the era of deterioration.

Much of the cathedral was damaged during the first Jacobite rising of 1689. After the battle of Killiecrankie, the victorious force of 3,000 Jacobite Highlanders advanced on Dunkeld, which was defended by the Cameronian Regiment, newly formed and with no battle experience. (The Cameronians were named after Richard Cameron, 'The Lion of the Covenant' – the Covenanters were upholders of the Presbyterian church, as opposed to the Episcopalian church which the Stuarts tried to impose on the Scots.) Under their commander, William Cleland, the Cameronians fortified the cathedral, and managed to drive the Highlanders back. Nearly all the houses in Dunkeld were burnt down during the battle, and the cathedral was damaged. At last the Highlanders ran for the hills, saying that their force could 'fight against men but was not fit to fight any more against devils'. Lieutenant Colonel Cleland, who had so ably defended Dunkeld, was killed in action and buried in the cathedral; but his Cameronians had helped to determine Scotland's future as a Presbyterian nation.

Above left: DUNKELD CATHEDRAL, FROM THE BRIDGE 1900   45945
Below left: DUNKELD CATHEDRAL, THE NAVE C1890   D655002

DUNKELD CATHEDRAL

FORTROSE ABBEY

Above: FORTROSE ABBEY C1880 F60301

Just off Fortrose's High Street in Cathedral Square stand the red sandstone ruins of Fortrose Cathedral. The cathedral dates from the reign of David I in the 1250s, when Bishop Robert chose this as the site for a new cathedral of Ross to replace St Peter's Church in Rosemarkie. Probably finished by 1300, it was never a vast or complex structure – it was about 185ft long and 25ft wide, with a south aisle, chapel and tower added in the 1400s. After the Reformation, the cathedral fell into ruin, the process hastened by the selling of the lead from the roof to Lord Ruthven in 1572. Then in the 1650s Cromwell's men took the stone from the ruinous nave and choir to construct his fort at Inverness; they did their job thoroughly – not even the pier bases survive. Thus all that is left is the south aisle and chapel (originally funded by Euphemia, Countess of Ross, whose tomb and effigy still lie within). Nearby is the sacristy and chapter house, which was used by the local council for meetings until the beginning of the Second World War.

INVERNESS CATHEDRAL

This cathedral church, in its exquisite setting alongside the River Ness, owes its existence to an Englishman, Robert Eden, who became Bishop of Moray and Ross in the 1850s. The building of a new cathedral was first suggested by the bishop in 1853. In 1866, the young architect and member of the congregation Alexander Ross put together the first designs. The foundation stone was laid by the Archbishop of Canterbury, and the building was completed in 1869.

Right: INVERNESS, THE NESS AND THE CATHEDRAL C1965 I25003

IONA ABBEY

'Iona of my heart, Iona of my love,
Instead of monks' voices there shall
be lowing of cattle:
But before the world comes to an end
Iona shall be as it was.'

So said St Columba (who founded a Christian community here in AD563) shortly before he died, according to St Adamnan in his 'Life of St Columba'. Indeed, although the monks endured here from the 6th to the 16th century (the Benedictines founded a monastery here in 1203), after the Reformation their voices were silent for a long time, and the abbey fell into ruin.

At last, at the beginning of the 20th century, the Duke of Argyll gave the abbey church to the Iona Cathedral Trust in the hope that restoration work might be undertaken; the building was eventually re-roofed, and used for worship again in 1910. In 1938, George Macleod founded the Iona Community and began the restoration of the buildings.

Today, modern pilgrims come in their thousands, and the Community lives, worships and teaches here, just as Columba's community and the Benedictine monks did in the past. The fascinating photograph 50889 (below left) shows the ruins as they were before restoration began – these are the ruins of the Benedictine monastery; little remains today of Columba's community. Nearer the camera is St Oran's chapel, dating from the 11th century; in the graveyard beside it, the oldest burial ground in Scotland, are the graves of 48 Scottish kings and chieftains, and the graves of kings of Ireland, France and Norway.

Left: IONA, THE ABBEY 1903 50889

The ruins are very different from those of most of the abbeys of England: instead of nestling in some sheltered dale, they stand on the wind-smitten shore of the bare and rocky isle; no groves of trees cluster around their grey walls, half-hiding them from the passer-by, nor does mantling ivy mask the rents which time and man have made. At Iona, the storm howls among its crumbling walls; its massive tower stands four square to all the winds that blow.

Victorian Guidebook

Above: IONA, THE BEACH AND THE VILLAGE 1903   50887

How many pilgrims has Iona's little harbour seen come and go? The scene in the photograph above looks little different today as modern travellers disembark from the ferry and set off on foot for the abbey (extreme right). By the roadside stands MacLean's Cross, an ancient marker showing pilgrims that their journey is nearly over, and in the abbey St Columba's cell can still be seen. But not everything here is centuries old; the rebuilt cloisters are ornamented with modern carvings, and in the centre of the cloister garth is a sculpture by Jacob Lipschitz, a holocaust survivor, representing peace on earth.

TOPICS

FRANCIS FRITH – Victorian pioneer

FRANCIS FRITH, *founder of the world-famous photographic archive, was a complex and multi-talented man. A devout Quaker and a highly successful Victorian businessman, he was philosophic by nature and pioneering in outlook. By 1855 he had already established a wholesale grocery business in Liverpool, and sold it for the astonishing sum of £200,000, which is the equivalent today of over £15,000,000. Now in his thirties, and captivated by the new science of photography, Frith set out on a series of pioneering journeys up the Nile and to the Near East.*

INTRIGUE AND EXPLORATION

He was the first photographer to venture beyond the sixth cataract of the Nile. Africa was still the mysterious 'Dark Continent', and Stanley and Livingstone's historic meeting was a decade into the future. The conditions for picture taking confound belief. He laboured for hours in his wicker dark-room in the sweltering heat of the desert, while the volatile chemicals fizzed dangerously in their trays. Back in London he exhibited his photographs and was 'rapturously cheered' by members of the Royal Society. His reputation as a photographer was made overnight.

VENTURE OF A LIFE-TIME

By the 1870s the railways had threaded their way across the country, and Bank Holidays and half-day Saturdays had been made obligatory by Act of Parliament. All of a sudden the working man and his family were able to enjoy days out, take holidays, and see a little more of the world.

With typical business acumen, Francis Frith foresaw that these new tourists would enjoy having souvenirs to commemorate their days out. For the next thirty years he travelled the country by train and by pony and trap, producing fine photographs of seaside resorts and beauty spots that were keenly bought by millions of Victorians. These prints were painstakingly pasted into family albums and pored over during the

dark nights of winter, rekindling precious memories of summer excursions. Frith's studio was soon supplying retail shops all over the country, and by 1890 F Frith & Co had become the greatest specialist photographic publishing company in the world, with over 2,000 sales outlets, and pioneered the picture postcard.

FRANCIS FRITH'S LEGACY

Francis Frith died in 1898, his great project still growing. The archive he created continued in business for another seventy years. By 1970 it contained over a third of a million pictures showing 7,000 British towns and villages.

Frith's legacy to us today is of immense significance and value, for the magnificent archive of evocative photographs he created provides a unique record of change in the cities, towns and villages throughout Britain over a century and more. Frith and his fellow studio photographers revisited locations many times down the years to update their views, compiling for us an enthralling and colourful pageant of British life and character.

We are fortunate that Frith was dedicated to recording the minutiae of everyday life. For it is this sheer wealth of visual data, the painstaking chronicle of changes in dress, transport, street layouts, buildings, housing, engineering and landscape that captivates us so much today, offering us a powerful link with the past and with the lives of our ancestors.

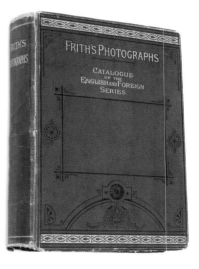

Computers now make Frith's images accessible almost instantly. The archive offers every one of us an opportunity to revisit the places where we and our families have lived and worked down the years. Its images, depicting our shared past, now bring pleasure and enlightenment to many millions, a century after Frith's death.

FREE PRINT OF YOUR CHOICE

Mounted Print
Overall size 14 x 11 inches (355 x 280mm)

CHOOSE A PHOTOGRAPH
FROM THIS BOOK

IMPORTANT!

These special prices are only available if you use this form to order.

You must use the ORIGINAL VOUCHER on this page (no copies permitted).

We can only despatch to one UK address.

This offer cannot be combined with any other offer.

Send completed voucher form to:
**The Francis Frith Collection,
Frith's Barn, Teffont, Salisbury,
Wiltshire SP3 5QP**

Choose any Frith photograph in this book.

Simply complete the voucher opposite and return it with your remittance for £3.50 (to cover postage and handling) and we will print the photograph of your choice in SEPIA (size 11 x 8 inches) and supply it in a cream mount with a burgundy rule line (overall size 14 x 11 inches).

Offer valid for delivery to UK addresses only.

***PLUS:* Order additional Mounted Prints at HALF PRICE - £7.49 each** (normally £14.99)

If you would like to order more Frith prints from this book, possibly as gifts for friends and family, you can buy them at half price (with no additional postage and handling costs).

***PLUS:* Have your Mounted Prints framed**

For an extra £14.95 per print you can have your mounted print(s) framed in an elegant polished wood and gilt moulding, overall size 16 x 13 inches (no additional postage and handling required).

Voucher for **FREE** *and Reduced Price Frith Prints*

Please do not photocopy this voucher. Only the original is valid, so please fill it in, cut it out and return it to us with your order.

Picture ref no	Page no	Qty	Mounted @ £7.49	Framed + £14.95	Total Cost £
		1	Free of charge*	£	£
			£7.49	£	£
			£7.49	£	£
			£7.49	£	£
			£7.49	£	£
			£7.49	£	£

Please allow 28 days for delivery.
Offer available to one UK address only

* Post & handling	£3.50
Total Order Cost	£

Title of this book . . . .

I enclose a cheque/postal order for £ . . . .
made payable to 'The Francis Frith Collection'

OR please debit my Mastercard / Visa / Maestro card, details below

Card Number

Issue No (Maestro only)   Valid from (Maestro)

Expires   Signature

Name Mr/Mrs/Ms . . . .

Address . . . .

. . . .

. . . .

. . . . Postcode . . . .

Daytime Tel No . . . .

Email . . . .

ISBN 1-84589-277-1   Valid to 31/12/09

Free Print – see overleaf

Can you help us with information about any of the Frith photographs in this book?

We are gradually compiling an historical record for each of the photographs in the Frith archive. It is always fascinating to find out the names of the people shown in the pictures, as well as insights into the shops, buildings and other features depicted.

If you recognize anyone in the photographs in this book, or if you have information not already included in the author's caption, do let us know. We would love to hear from you, and will try to publish it in future books or articles.

Our production team

Frith books are produced by a small dedicated team at offices in the converted Grade II listed 18th-century barn at Teffont near Salisbury, illustrated above. Most have worked with The Francis Frith Collection for many years. All have in common one quality: they have a passion for The Francis Frith Collection. The team is constantly expanding, but currently includes:

Andrew Alsop, Paul Baron, Jason Buck, John Buck, Jenny Coles, Heather Crisp, David Davies, Natalie Davis, Louis du Mont, Isobel Hall, Chris Hardwick, Julian Hight, Peter Horne, James Kinnear, Karen Kinnear, Tina Leary, Stuart Login, Sue Molloy, Sarah Roberts, Kate Rotondetto, Eliza Sackett, Terence Sackett, Sandra Sampson, Adrian Sanders, Sandra Sanger, Julia Skinner, Lewis Taylor, Will Tunnicliffe, David Turner and Ricky Williams.